Counselling
with
Reality
Therapy

For Hiroko,
Bob Wubbolding
2/25/09

Titles in the **Speechmark Editions** series:

Counselling
with
Reality
Therapy

Robert E Wubbolding
& John Brickell

Published by
Speechmark Publishing Ltd, 8 Oxford Court, St James Road, Brackley NN13 7XY, United Kingdom
Telephone: +44 (0) 1280 845570   Fax: +44 (0) 1280 845584
www.speechmark.net

002-3114/Printed in the United Kingdom/1010

British Library Cataloguing in Publication Data
Wubbolding, Robert E
  Counselling with reality therapy
  1. Reality therapy   2. Counselling
  I. Title   II. Brickell, John
  361'.06

ISBN 978 0 86388 338 5

(Previously published by Winslow Press Ltd under ISBN 0 86388 215 3)

To my wife, Sandie, with whom I belong, have fun and enjoy life.

Robert Wubbolding

To the most needs-satisfying people in my life: Margaret, Maura and Kate; and to my parents, Eileen and Jim and my brother Les.

John Brickell

Contents

Figures

About the Authors

Robert E Wubbolding EdD, internationally known teacher, author and practitioner of Reality Therapy, has taught Choice Theory and Reality Therapy in the United States, Europe, the Middle East and Asia. His focus has been upon teaching therapists, counsellors, educators, managers and others in the UK for ten years. His contributions to the theory and practice include 'The Cycle of Counselling' and the 'Five Levels of Commitment', and he has also expanded significantly the procedure of 'evaluation'. He has written extensively on Reality Therapy in various British journals. Among his publications are: *Using Reality Therapy*; *Understanding Reality Therapy*; *Employee Motivation* and *Reality Therapy with Children*.

His busy professional life includes being an advisory associate to the Centre for Reality Therapy (UK), in Leighton Buzzard, England as well as being professor of counselling at Xavier University in Cincinnati, Ohio. Additionally as Director of Training for The William Glasser Institute in Chatsworth, California, he monitors the Certification Process and the Instructor Training Programme.

John Brickell DC is Director of the Centre for Reality Therapy (UK), a senior faculty member of The William Glasser Institute, California, and is Director of Training for The William Glasser Institute (UK). He has taught Reality Therapy in the USA, the Middle East, the Far East and in several European countries as well as throughout the UK.

As an independent counsellor, John also has experience in working with alcohol and drug addictions, and as a trainer/consultant specializes in stress management, coaching and self-esteem programmes. As well as working for several major UK companies, he has for the past 12 years been an associate lecturer at Ashridge Management College, in Hertfordshire.

More recently, he qualified as a McTimoney chiropractor which, as well as providing some 'backbone' to the other areas in which he works, also complements the mind-body approach of Reality Therapy. Along with Robert Wubbolding, he has written articles on Reality Therapy for several British journals and is co-author of *A Set of Directions, For Putting and Keeping Yourself Together*.

Introduction

THIS BOOK provides a jargon-free and practical explanation of a theory and method of counselling which can be used in any therapeutic relationship. It also contains ideas which can be used by parents, spouses, supervisors, teachers and anyone wishing for more satisfying relationships.

The theory is based on one simple proposition: we choose our behaviour in order to satisfy our inner needs at any given moment. This statement appears simple and commonsensical, but it transcends all human relationships and challenges, conventional psychology, treatment philosophy and educational practice.

Frequently we hear people say that they do not wish to control others and that such regulation of others' behaviour is impossible. They then proceed to reward and punish children, students and employees with external incentives. Choice Theory, the underlying theory of brain functioning and human motivation, challenges the 'external control psychology' that is explicit or implicit in so many corollaries and conclusions which are important in helping people reach a higher level of happiness. To be more specific, the needs which motivate people are survival, belonging, power, fun and freedom. When these are fulfilled, a person is said to be well adjusted and happy; when they are unmet or met in destructive ways, the person might experience pleasure but not genuine happiness. Behaviour, according to Choice Theory, is holistic or 'total' and made up of action, thinking, feeling and physiology. Difficult as it is to accept, most of these are choices. And even if a counsellor does not believe that these are selected by clients, treatment is hastened when they are dealt with *as if* they were chosen. The reader is encouraged to accept at this point at least that human beings have more control than they think they have.

The delivery system of Reality Therapy is best expressed in the acronym WDEP. This is a system which can be learned and retained by counsellors as well as taught to clients. Each of the letters symbolizes, not one idea, but a cluster of ideas explained in subsequent chapters. In summary, W = Exploration of *Wants*, D = Discussion of *Doing* or all four aspects of behaviour, E = Helping clients *Evaluate* their own behaviour, and P = Formulating a specific, attainable *Plan* of action.

You are encouraged to view the ideas in this book as information to be used or discarded as you see fit. In fact we urge you to use the ideas in your own lives first, then try them with clients. If these ideas and concepts help you, use them with others. If they do not work for you, do not use them with anyone else. We are quite confident about what happens when people start to live Choice Theory and implement the WDEP system.

After you have read this book, used the ideas on yourself and applied them to clients, we ask you to write to the authors to provide feedback. We are committed to the principles of W Edwards Deming, the prophet of quality who spoke of continuous improvement as a means of trying to reach the ever-moving target of quality. Your comments will help us in our quest for quality.

Robert E Wubbolding
John Brickell

CHAPTER 1

History of Reality Therapy*

IN THE WORLD OF therapy and education, Reality Therapy preceded Choice Theory. It was after many years of practice that the theory justifying Reality Therapy emerged.

William Glasser created Reality Therapy on the basis of his experience with clients. Almost all of his training, however, came from conventional psychoanalysis. As the concepts of Reality Therapy emerged, Glasser rebelled against his formal training, noticing that many of his teachers did not practise what they taught. As they demonstrated by their interactions with clients, he noticed that what seemed to work was not what was said to work. What was actually done in effective therapy was often much closer to what later became Reality Therapy.

One of Glasser's few non-analytical teachers, GL Harrington, encouraged him to put his ideas into practice and to discuss his thoughts. Harrington became Glasser's mentor and helped him to formalize Reality Therapy in the early 1960s. Harrington himself was influenced by Helmuth Kaiser, a psychoanalyst with whom he had worked in the 1950s at the Menninger Clinic, and who also had begun to turn away from conventional analysis.

Early Reality Therapy
Reality Therapy began when Glasser became dissatisfied with psychoanalytic psychiatry as taught at the Veterans Administration, Brentwood Hospital and at the University of California at Los Angeles.

---

*Adapted from Glasser & Wubbolding (1995).

1

What disturbed him most were the endless ruminations about how the client's behaviour was 'caused' by others in the client's family or by a 'harsh' world. Clients were generally seen as victims of forces beyond their control and the role of the analyst was to give them insight into their unconscious so that they could regroup and cope. Even when clients gained insight after insight, and when transferences were worked through, all too often they stayed the same or even became worse, taking less responsibility for what they did.

On his own, Glasser began to focus on the present and to try to get clients to realize that they were responsible for what they did, that they had to change themselves and that they could not count on others to change or help them, no matter how much insight they gained. For example, one woman had been attending the clinic for three years and had spent most of that time blaming her nervousness and depression on her now-dead grandfather. Glasser told her that he would see her only on the condition that she could never again mention her grandfather. She was shocked and responded, 'If I don't talk about my grandfather, what will I talk about?' Glasser told her to talk about what she was doing now in her life to solve her problems, because her grandfather was dead and no longer had anything to do with her life. In a few short months, even with this early crude version of Reality Therapy, the woman stopped 'depressing' and 'anxietising' (Choice Theory behaviour terms) and started doing many things to fulfil her needs. She had taken control of her own life by making more effective choices. For three years, traditional therapy had deprived her of the chance to help herself.

O'Donnell (1987) described how Glasser timidly explained this unorthodox move to his residency consultant, GL Harrington. Instead of reprimanding Glasser, Harrington shook his hand and said, 'Join the club.' This started a seven-year relationship during which Harrington continued to consult with Glasser and helped him formulate the ideas that became Reality Therapy.

In 1965, Glasser became consultant to the Ventura School, a California Youth Authority institution for delinquent girls, where the young women had all been told that they were emotionally disturbed and were not responsible for their lawbreaking. The people who ran the school were upset at this view and supported Glasser in his attempt to introduce the beginnings of Reality Therapy into this and other Youth Authority institutions.

Current Reality Therapy

At present, Reality Therapy is recognized as an effective therapeutic modality with many applications. For example, an unpublished document of the United States Department of Defense, used at a 1981 conference on drug abuse in the armed forces, stated that over 90 per cent of the more than 200 armed forces clinics that treat drug and alcohol abuse use Reality Therapy as their preferred therapeutic approach.

Much of the work of practitioners of Reality Therapy extends beyond the world of psychotherapy. In 1968, Glasser wrote *Schools Without Failure*, in which he asserted that, when children are unable to control their world successfully (that is, to succeed in school), it hurts so much that they often stop trying to learn. At the present time, The William Glasser Institute and its instructors teach the concepts in Glasser's *The Quality School* (1990) to schools in the United States and elsewhere. In this ground-breaking work, Glasser applied many of the ideas of W Edwards Deming (1984) to education. The major problem underlying the educational system is not the disruption of the students, poorly paid teachers, unused computers, lack of community involvement or any of the dozens of other problems. Rather, these problems are symptoms of the simple but overlooked fact that Americans had settled for mediocre work, behaviour and efforts on the part of students. If education is at risk, it is due to the lack of quality education. Glasser believes that Choice Theory and Reality Therapy, if taught properly, can enhance the quality of performance in schools. In a 'Quality School', everyone has been trained to use the principles of Deming and Glasser. Schools interested in these principles have formed a consortium numbering, in 1998, well over 200 schools.

Still, Reality Therapy remains the counselling and therapy tool that it was from the very beginning. It is taught in many countries besides the United States, Canada and the United Kingdom. The William Glasser Institute has ties to Japan, Korea, Ireland, Norway, the United Kingdom, Australia, New Zealand, Hong Kong, Singapore, Italy, Croatia, Slovenia, Kuwait, Spain and France.

Since the publication of Glasser's *Stations of the Mind* (1981) and *Control Theory* (1984), thousands of people have heard about Choice Theory and its delivery system, Reality Therapy. Moreover, Glasser (1990) has reconceptualized the essentials of Reality Therapy under two general categories: environment and procedures. Robert Wubbolding (1992) has extended these ideas by describing them as a 'cycle of therapy' and the 'WDEP system' (Wants, Doing, Evaluation and Planning). Robert Cockrum (1989) stated, 'William Glasser has never been content to allow his theories to be taught or used without constant scrutiny, addition and sometimes even major changes.' These concepts are the subject of this book.

In 1981, *The Journal of Reality Therapy* was launched, edited by Lawrence Litwack. Since that time, more than 250 essays, articles and research studies have been published on the applications of Reality Therapy. By 1998, nearly 4,500 people had completed the Reality Therapy certification process worldwide, with the numbers increasing each year. Reality Therapy has seen a slow but steady increase in acceptance as a viable and respected method of counselling/psychotherapy, as a theory and as an educational system.

CHAPTER 2

Choice Theory: The Psychology Underlying Reality Therapy

THE UNDERLYING PSYCHOLOGY described in this chapter is based on a long-standing theory of brain functioning which is rooted more in the field of engineering than in psychology. Norbert Wiener (1948), who coined the word 'cybernetics', described the importance of both information and feedback in engineering and in biological systems. He later (1950) described the sociological implications. Other major contributors to the development of the theory include William Sickles (1976) and Gordon Pask (1976).

William Glasser was most proximately influenced by the work of William Powers (1973). In Powers' opinion, 'Control Theory' provides a true-to-life alternative to the 'mechanistic formalisms' of behaviourism. Glasser (1981; 1984) added to this theory by incorporating psychological principles and by using it as a clinical and educational model. It is now applied to counselling, psychotherapy, education, management, parenting and virtually every human relationship, and is made operational through the principles of Reality Therapy, the focus of this chapter.

Basic Principles of Choice Theory

Glasser (1986) has stated that human beings are driven to behave. Human behaviour originates from within a person, not from outside stimuli. Whether this behaviour is effective or ineffective, it is aimed at manoeuvring the external world so that human needs and wants are fulfilled. More specifically, Choice Theory, as used by practitioners of Reality Therapy can be summarised in four principles, (i) Needs, (ii) Wants, (iii) Behaviour and (iv) Perceptions, described below.

In 1996 Glasser (*Programs, Policies and Procedures of The William Glasser Institute*, 1996) changed the name of the theory. Because many changes have been made in the original Control Theory, the current view of human behaviour is quite different from the 'Control Theory' of Powers and others. The theory has progressed beyond the abstractions of the control theorists. Glasser has formulated a clinical and an educational mode. In fact the theory and its delivery system, Reality Therapy, are applicable to virtually all human relationships.

In her book, *The Fountainhead*, Ayn Rand (1943) says, 'Throughout history there were men who took first steps down new roads armed with nothing but their vision.' William Glasser, MD, the founder of Reality Therapy, is such a person. Trained in the traditional methods of psychiatry, he came to the conclusion early in his career that even though many clients gained insight and dealt with transference, there was too often little change in their behaviour, particularly in the longer term. Conversely, by helping clients to take responsibility for their behavioural choices rather than accepting they were victims of their own impulses, their past history, or of other people or circumstances around them, they were able to make dramatic changes. In 1965 Glasser published *Reality Therapy, A New Approach to Psychiatry*, a controversial book for its time.

Glasser was not the first to say that therapy should include an effort to teach, encourage and help people take responsibility for their behaviour. Helmut Kaiser (1965) also spoke of the importance of personal responsibility in therapeutic change. Earlier, Alfred Adler had written extensively about the fact that human behaviour is teleological, that is, it has a purpose which originates within a person (Whitehouse, 1984).

Others have attempted to extend Glasser's ideas to the field of self-help (Wubbolding, 1990a), relationships (Ford, 1977; 1979; 1983; Cockrum, 1994; Glasser, 1995; Wubbolding, 1990b), burnout (Edelwich, 1980; Wubbolding, 1979), stress management (Brickell, 1992), school discipline and classroom management (Wubbolding,

1993), coaching employees (Wubbolding, 1984; 1990c), educational reform (Greene, 1995; Hoglund, 1993) and addictions (Wubbolding, 1985; Brickell & Wubbolding, 1995; 1996).

Needs

The ultimate, most fundamental source of human motivation is the internal system of human needs. Because the system is internal, it is controlled neither by external forces nor by past experiences. This principle is in direct opposition to what Glasser (1998) refers to as 'external control psychology' or the 'pop behaviourism' described by Alfie Kohn (1993a).

As Robert Cockrum, a senior instructor in Reality Therapy, frequently points out, the needs are 'undeniable'. All behaviour ultimately is an attempt to fulfil one or more of the needs. Similarly, the needs are genetic and universal; all human beings have needs. The implications of this characteristic have not yet been fully explored, but it is clear that all people, regardless of colour, gender, race, age or experience, are united because of common needs. Thus the human needs system crosses all cultures. More specifically, there are five categories of needs and many levels of intensity within each need. The needs are (1) survival, (2) love and belonging, (3) power/self-worth, (4) freedom and (5) fun and enjoyment; that is, one physiological and four psychological needs.

It is important here to mention that, unlike Abraham Maslow's well known developmental model of motivation (Maslow, 1943), the needs are not in an ascending hierarchy, although, of course, most of the time we will choose survival ahead of the other needs. However, if it were true that human beings always satisfied their need for survival first, it would follow that there would be no suicide. Indeed, research has shown that by far the commonest reason for people to commit suicide or attempt it is desperate loneliness (the need for love and belonging).

It is not surprising, then, that Glasser states so strongly that the most prominent need is for love and belonging, and that this is the one which Reality Therapists should concentrate on most in their practice. Having said that, let us look at each of the needs in turn.

Survival

This is our basic physiological need: to survive as individuals and reproduce so that we survive as a species. It includes our physical needs for food, water, air, safety, shelter, warmth, physical health and hormone-driven sex. Obviously, there can also be other genetic motivations for sex, such as love, power, fun and enjoyment, and, perhaps, also freedom. No wonder, then, with the possibility of all five needs being involved, that the human sex drive can be so strong and long-lasting!

Survival also extends to the need for a sense of security in respect of the on-going provision of these basic needs. Invariably, this means having sufficient income to pay for them.

Love and Belonging

This is our psychological need to love and care for others and, importantly, to believe that we are loved and cared about ourselves. It includes family relationships, friendships, working relationships and acquaintanceships that provide us with a sense of belonging and 'connectedness' with people.

In his book, *Choice Theory: A New Psychology of Personal Freedom* (Glasser, 1998) Glasser emphasizes the importance of this need by stating that unsatisfactory or non-existent 'connections' with people are the source of almost all long-term human problems. Therefore a major goal in counselling with Reality Therapy is to help clients 'connect' or 'reconnect' with the people they care about, are involved with, or want to be closer to.

Further, the emphasis, as stated by Glasser, of 'disconnectedness' being inherent in the vast majority of human problems extends to all settings and relationships, whether it be between couples, parents and children, in families, in social settings, work relationships, or in schools and education. Whatever the presenting problem, 'disconnectedness', according to Glasser, will be an underlying cause or issue.

Power/Self-Worth

This is the need for a sense of empowerment, worthiness, self-efficacy and achievement. Power does not imply the exploitation of or dominance over another person. It is similar to the meaning of the French word 'pouvoir': to be able, to be capable. Even though the need for power leads many people to wish to compete, the need is not limited to winning. More fundamentally, it is an inner sense of self-actualization, a condition of inner control. It implies a sense of achievement, accomplishment, pride, importance and self-esteem, all of which need not be measured by someone else's behaviour.

Freedom
The third psychological need is that of freedom. It is the need for independence and autonomy: the ability to make choices, to create, to explore and to express oneself freely; to have sufficient space, to move around and to feel unrestricted in determination of choices and free will.

Kohn (1993b) has documented the results attained in education by allowing students to make choices, thus fulfilling their inner need for freedom.

Fun and Enjoyment
The fourth psychological need, but not the least important, is that of fun or enjoyment. Aristotle once defined a human being as a creature that is 'risible'. It can laugh. Fun is thus a very philosophical notion. The Greeks spoke of one of the virtues as 'Eutropelia' or having fun. The desire to enjoy a job, to have a sense of humour even about serious events, to engage in a hobby, to have interest and to feel excitement about a work project or a leisure time activity springs from the need for fun or enjoyment. Furthermore, fun is the internal payoff for learning (Glasser, 1998).

The human need system is always in operation urging human beings to generate behaviours. It is innate, always up-to-date, universal, and thus can be a unifying force for humankind.

Specific Wants: The Quality World
Human beings, united by the innate and all-pervading system of needs, develop specific wants. Each person, as they grow, interacting with family and culture, develops specific and unique wants as to how the

needs are to be met. We have wants related to each need. These are analogous to pictures in that each one is specific. This extensive collection of pictures or wants has been called a 'mental picture album' (Glasser, 1984) and more recently the 'quality world' (Glasser, 1990; 1995; 1998). All elements in the quality world are seen as desirable and thus have quality. They are seen as need-satisfying, not harmful, meeting an inner standard, and in some way beneficial.

When a person chooses a specific behaviour to fulfil a need and to satisfy a want at a given moment, it is the result of a discrepancy, a gap, sometimes labelled a 'frustration', between what the person has and what the person wants. Thus, if someone is thirsty (survival), wants a glass of water, and perceives that they do not have a glass, there is motivation to walk to a pitcher, pour water into a glass and drink it. Consequently, the mental scale (frustration) is put back in balance.

The question here might be: 'How does this motivational system relate to counselling or education?' There are several implications. The first task of the helper is to attempt *to be part of the quality world of the client*. This is accomplished through the effective use of Reality Therapy. Also many people live each day with many out-of-balance scales, that is, many differences between what they want and what they are getting. The helper's task is to assist them to get what they want, and to choose behaviours that are truly more effective than those chosen in the past. Finally, some clients, such as those addicted to drugs, do not have an 'out-of-balance scale'. They do not see the need for change. They believe everyone else has a problem. They often think they are getting what they want. The helper's function is, in this case, *to help them get their scales out of balance* and thus develop more effective behaviours for fulfilling their needs. The helper's job is at times to 'comfort the afflicted' and at other times to 'afflict the comfortable'.

Human Behaviour
Human behaviour, originating from the gap between 'wants' and 'gots' is composed of action, thinking, feeling, and physiology and is thus referred to as 'total behaviour'.

Total behaviour is often described as a car which functions as a unit. The front wheels are action and thinking and the back wheels are feeling and physiology. All behaviour is constructed from these four components and none can exist without the others. The direction of most cars is controlled by the front wheels. Similarly, a human being has more choices regarding the action and thinking component than over the back wheels of feeling and physiology. Because of the emphasis on thinking and action, Reality Therapy, the delivery system of Choice Theory, is appropriately called a comprehensive cognitive behavioural therapy, in that all elements are treated but emphasis is placed on the cognitive and action elements. Another analogy useful in understanding total behaviour is that of the 'suitcase of behaviour' (Wubbolding, 1991). In the suitcase are four levels of behaviour: action, thinking, feeling and physiology. The handle on the top is attached to the action level.

The practical point of these analogies is represented by the axiom, 'You can act your way to a new way of thinking more easily than you can think your way to a new way of acting.' Even though there is emphasis on the thinking component, as when therapists help clients conduct self-evaluations, the goal is to assist them to make more effective plans for life changes.

The behavioural components are seen as inseparable, though one of them is often more prominent than the others. Feelings might be more noticeable at a given time. Combining these two aspects of total behaviour, visibility and inseparability has led Glasser (1984; 1998) to use 'ing' words to describe even feelings and physiology. People are said to be 'guilting', 'depressing', 'anxietising', 'angering', 'headaching', 'ulcering' and so on. Such behaviours are seen, not as static conditions thrust upon us from the outside, but as behaviours originating within.

Consequently, the user of Reality Therapy assists the client to *steer the car* in a more effective direction, to insert new behaviours into the suitcase, and to transport the suitcase to more desirable locations by lifting it by the handle. These efforts are described as choices and are treated as such by the counsellor.

Perception

Human beings see the world through a perceptual system and retain perceptions in their 'perceived world', an inner storehouse of memories. More specifically, human beings want the perception of having needs and wants fulfilled. We only know what we perceive. The incoming images received from the world pass through sensory receptors and then through the human psychological perceptual system. As they pass through the lower filter in the perceptual system they are simply recognized and labelled. It is here that we acknowledge the world around us. This lower filter is known as the 'total knowledge filter'. A person entering a meeting room in a hotel sees hundreds of chairs and simply labels them chairs. They are recognized and labelled in a way that society has agreed upon. They are chairs. The images then proceed through a higher level filter called the 'valuing filter'. The perceptions receive a positive, negative or neutral value. If the chairs are uncomfortable, they receive a negative value, perhaps an increasingly negative value as the day wears on. On the other hand, when the same person returns home and sits in a chair that has been in the family for generations and is thus an heirloom, a positive value is attached to the chair.

Human beings seek perceptions. They want the perception of being attractive, of being competent, of being a good parent, of having good health, of being in control, of being secure or rich, or strong, popular, happy. The list of possible desirable and undesirable perceptions is unlimited.

The perceptions are stored in a 'mental file cabinet'. Some are seen as satisfying needs, some as threats to need fulfilment and some as neutral. Because the file cabinet, the 'perceived world', contains perceptions which are *desirable*, it is said to be the repository of the quality world.

Thus the system is indeed a loop. Behaviour is the output generated to gain the input of perceptions that satisfy wants and needs. The brain clearly functions in a way similar to a temperature control system. The thermostat 'wants' the room at 72 degrees. It compares what it wants with what it perceives it is getting from the world around it. When it perceives the room temperature at 78 degrees it sends a signal to its behaviour system, the air conditioning unit, to take action to manoeuvre the external world so that the 'wants' of the thermostat can be met. The thermostat generates behaviour which can be quite effective. It could, of course, be ineffective if someone kept the windows of the house open, thus making it impossible for the thermostat to fulfil its purposes.

Many human beings also generate behaviour which is effective and at times ineffective. The goal of the counsellor using Reality Therapy is to help clients choose and even create helpful behaviours from a range of possibilities much wider than that of a thermostat. This is accomplished by the relentless, determined, empathic and skilful use of techniques and procedural interventions described in this book.

CHAPTER 3

Creating the Counselling Relationship (I)

Introduction

As previously stated, Reality Therapy is similar to some theories but very different from many others, and this is most certainly true with regard to creating the counselling relationship (otherwise referred to as the counselling environment or therapeutic alliance).

In some of the more conventional psychiatric approaches (following the influence of Freud), the therapist is taught to remain as impersonal and objective as possible, regarded by some observers as being somewhat 'aloof' from the client. By contrast, in Reality Therapy the creation of effective 'involvement' – a term used frequently by Glasser – is regarded as absolutely essential to the counselling process. Indeed, as Glasser states, the more the counsellor can become someone whom the client comes to put into their 'quality world', as a professional person whom they trust and who has their best interests at heart, the more effective the counselling process can be.

To establish a counselling relationship conducive to positive change, the guidelines which follow have proved very effective, although it should be stressed that they are *suggestions* or *guidelines* and not rigid 'must do's'. Indeed, many of these guidelines should have the words 'appropriately' and 'sometimes' in parentheses, because they will always need to be utilized according to the client's particular circumstances and, of course, in consideration of the particular situation. Bear in mind that Reality Therapy is practised in many different therapeutic settings as well as in environments where managing, supervising or coaching people (in schools, business or agencies) is required.

Additionally, it should be emphasized that, no matter what the setting, the 'involvement' or relationship referred to here is always kept within professional boundaries and ethical standards. Although this should go without saying, it should nevertheless not go without saying!

The guidelines which follow have been written by Wubbolding elsewhere (1988; 1994) and are illustrated in the 'Cycle of Counselling' (see Figure 1) and can be regarded as some things to do and some things to avoid. This forms the bottom rectangle in the 'Cycle of Counselling' figure, referred to as the environment. The purpose of this rectangle is to convey the idea of a foundation stone, upon which the procedures which lead to effective change can be built.

Additionally, it should be emphasized that the culmination of practising the 'do's' and 'don'ts' is creating a relationship based on *trust* (see Figure 1). Achieving this requires the counsellor to be appropriately *firm*, *fair* and *friendly*: the three 'F's beneath the word 'trust' in the figure. Building such trust as well as rapport is something that the counsellor endeavours to do from the very first contact with the client (perhaps over the phone) and is also something that will invariably have to be 'earned' over time, particularly with hostile or resistant clients.

The reader should be aware that creating the counselling relationship is not something which comes first: before using the procedures that lead to change. Rather, in most cases they happen simultaneously. However, on some occasions with very hostile or resistant clients, building trust is vital before the counselling procedures can be implemented. Hence the broken line separating environment and procedures in the figure, indicating that the two components are sometimes separate but on most occasions are intertwined.

Creating the Counselling Relationship

As mentioned previously, in Reality Therapy the development of an authentic, warm and trusting relationship is regarded as essential to effective counselling. The Cycle of Counselling provides suggestions or guidelines that can help to build this relationship (referred to as the 'do's') and some to avoid (the 'don'ts'). The present chapter addresses the 'do's'.

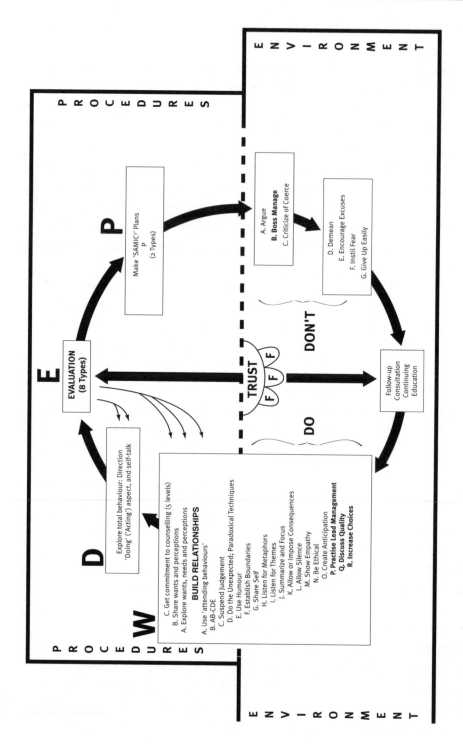

Figure 1 *Cycle of Managing, Supervising, Counselling and Coaching using Reality Therapy*

Source: Adapted by Robert E Wubbolding from the works of William Glasser

© 1986 Robert E Wubbolding, 10th Revision, 1998

A *Use Attending Behaviours*

Rather than simply refer to 'attentive listening', the idea of 'attending behaviours' seems more appropriate because we are really implying listening with the entire body. This includes adopting an open and receptive sitting position; eye contact and facial expression, that is, looking at the client without staring, and displaying genuine interest; following the client's comments and reflecting them back in a manner that conveys understanding by the counsellor; other non-verbal behaviours, such as 'reading' the client's manner of expression, such as pitch and tone of voice; and paraphrasing: feeding back the client's comments, occasionally but not *ad nauseam*.

B *Practise the ABs (AB:CDE)*

In attempting to develop a friendly but professional relationship with clients, our guidelines also suggest practising the ABs (AB = always be).

Always Be Courteous

Demonstrating what Carl Rogers referred to as unconditional positive regard for the client is echoed in Reality Therapy, even if the client is angry or abusive – often easier said than done, of course. The counsellor attempts to remain courteous, calm and unintimidated despite the upset displayed by the client.

It is important for the counsellor to allow clients to express their upset or angry feelings, recognizing that displaying such emotions is the best possible choice at that time, as far as the client sees it. Looking at the upset or 'angering' with understanding and in a, perhaps, more rational and non-judgemental way is most certainly not easy, but can often be very helpful to the client because it demonstrates the acceptance and respect for the client irrespective of the behaviours they may demonstrate.

Always Be Determined

In teaching Reality Therapy to counsellors, Glasser has often said that a message to be communicated to clients is, 'this is a 'work-it-out' office'. In other words, the counsellor should be determined to help clients 'work out' their problems and issues no matter how difficult they might appear to be.

As previously stated, a major principle in Reality Therapy is that behaviours are almost always chosen and, further, that more helpful and need-fulfilling behavioural choices are almost always available; irrespective of how difficult the client's situation might be or how limited their immediate number of choices may appear. As a consequence of this attitude, Reality Therapy has frequently been described as an optimistic approach and this is certainly the case. Wubbolding constantly conveys in his teaching the importance of communicating a sense of *hope* to the client (Wubbolding, 1996): that life can be better in the future and does not have to be a repetition of past misery.

This attitude or belief is, of course, idealistic and such ideals are not attained 100 per cent of the time by 100 per cent of those reaching for them, but it is an extremely positive and powerful belief that can be crucial, not only to the counselling relationship but arguably to the successful outcome of the counselling itself.

Wubbolding (1986) cites the case of a woman who had been 'depressing' for many years and who throughout the first counselling session continued to sob and cry about her unhappy past and present relationships. The following week, when she appeared for the second session, there were no more tears and she seemed quite cheerful. When asked how she came to seem so much brighter, the client said, 'You just assumed my depression would be temporary.' Wubbolding responded, 'The thought never occurred to me that it could be permanent.'

Always Be Enthusiastic
The enthusiasm referred to here is strongly linked to the above attitude of 'always be determined'. However, this does not suggest a 'rah, rah, rah', 'you can do it' approach but rather that the counsellor conveys a positive and enthusiastic attitude towards the actual counselling session itself. The counsellor should do this irrespective of whether they are having a 'good day' or a 'bad day'. The ability to put one's own emotions or issues 'on hold' and to be totally present with the client is essential to effective counselling, but, more than this, to communicate the sense of positiveness and enthusiasm which we are referring to

here is invariably to provide a necessary, perhaps a crucial stimulus to the client's readiness to make some changes in their life.

C *Suspend Judgement*

One guideline that is accepted as an ethical boundary is to refrain from judging the client. Thus counsellors should avoid commenting on clients' thoughts, actions and/or statements that produce consternation or may serve as points of contention. Instead, counsellors should wait to discuss this material until the next session, when the client–counsellor interaction over such material will undoubtedly be more productive.

Counsellors can occasionally show disapproval of destructive actions, but their overall stance should be one of *acceptance*. This implies that the counsellor is able to see the client's behaviours from a 'low level of perception' that is, without judging or condemning. This requires that the counsellor be able to view even the destructive behaviours of clients as their best efforts to fulfil their needs. The converse of this guideline is to view clients' behaviour from a 'high level of perception'; that is, to put a value (approval or disapproval) on clients' best efforts.

D *Do the Unexpected*

As with some of the other 'do's', this guideline is one that needs to be used appropriately and occasionally in the attempt to build relationships based on trust and to help the client undertake positive change. Doing the unexpected becomes 'appropriate' in particular when clients are actively or passively resistant to change. The intention is to help put the counselling process onto a more positive or constructive footing.

This also touches on the subject of using paradoxical techniques (appropriately and on occasions) which, because of their highly interactive nature, are very applicable in the practice of Reality Therapy. One example of this could be to 'positively reframe' (a paradoxical technique) the client's negative experiences. For instance, an angry person could be told, 'At least you are clear about how you feel.' The intention here would be to endeavour to build on something more positive, rather than focusing on negative or destructive behaviours which may have been unproductively explored with the client several times in previous counselling sessions. In this example, focusing on the positive (reframe) would, most likely, be regarded by the client as 'unexpected', and, it is hoped, would help to put the counselling process on a more constructive track.

Other examples of doing the unexpected are for the counsellor to respond in an unexpected way. For example, in addictions counselling, the client no doubt expects the counsellor to (yet again) discuss failure behaviours such as the steps that led to relapse, past problems and the like. Unexpectedly, the counsellor discusses successful positive behaviours. Instead of asking, 'Why did you take drugs?' the counsellor asks, 'When was the last time you had fun and enjoyed yourself without getting into trouble and without taking drugs?' In family counselling, there is a tendency to focus on one member who is the 'identified client'. It can often be helpful to spend a session in which the counsellor focuses on everyone except the 'identified client'. Again, the intention here would be to help put the counselling process on a more constructive track, when the counsellor perceives it may become stuck if past failure or miseries are rehashed yet again and/or when resistance is anticipated.

E *Use Humour Whenever Appropriate*

Used occasionally and appropriately by the counsellor, humour can be of great benefit to the client, particularly when they have been 'down in the dumps' for a long time. However, such humour should always be good-natured and never sarcastic, critical or patronizing. It should be well timed and perhaps point out some human foible or incongruity. It should help both the client and the counsellor laugh and learn and help to 'lighten the load'.

Obviously, there are many situations in which humour would be counterproductive, for example any situation in which grief or loss was an issue. However, in general, when used appropriately, humour can help strengthen the relationship between the counsellor and the client; as the comedian Victor Borge once said, 'The shortest distance between two people is a laugh.' There is also great truth in the saying that laughter is the best medicine.

F *Establish Boundaries*

As well as adhering to ethical guidelines (see *Be Ethical*, p25) it is essential to establish boundaries in the client–counsellor relationship, which in essence is providing some structure in the counselling session. Examples of this would be informing the client of what you *will* and *will not* do and clarifying responsibilities: for instance, informing the client that you will help them come up with some possible plans which they can choose to implement thereafter, but that you will not make that choice for them – the responsibility remains with them; or, perhaps, if counselling in a probation setting, telling the client that you will be willing to write a favourable reference/report to the court, but that you are not willing to write any lies. Their responsibility is to 'earn' the favourable report.

G *Share Yourself and be Yourself*

Share yourself. The very idea of 'sharing oneself' in the counselling relationship would be criticized and opposed in some counselling theories and particularly so in the context of the seemingly austere 'distance' maintained in conventional psychiatry. Therefore it is important to emphasize that this is a suggested guideline and not a 'must do'. Reality Therapy can still be practised effectively without adherence to this guideline.

However, the idea which we intend to convey here is that self-disclosure, when used sparingly (in other words, appropriately and on occasion), can enhance the therapeutic relationship without damaging the necessary therapeutic distance which it is essential to maintain. As Carl Rogers once stated, 'Self-disclosure is the greatest form of empathy.' So perhaps our concern is really a matter of degree and timing: how much self-disclosure and when is it appropriate?

Wubbolding (1986) has suggested that the counselling relationship 'has reached a higher level when the client begins to ask the therapist a few questions about his or her life'. The desire of the client is to know a little more about the counsellor as a human being but invariably not going much deeper than the superficial details of whether they are married or single, or if they have children of their own, or maybe some of their career history. Obviously, it would be very inappropriate for the counsellor/therapist to disclose any information about their most intimate affairs, personal problems and so on. So, again, the concern here is very much one of degree.

Be yourself. It is important to emphasize that the practice of Reality Therapy should be adapted to the counsellor's own personality and style. There is no one style that is necessarily better than another, although of course there is a most valuable skill in being able to adapt one's style sometimes in consideration of the client's own personality and the particular counselling setting.

Having said that, the importance of 'being yourself' is something that we continuously emphasize in our training in the skills of Reality Therapy.

H *Listen for Metaphors*

Clients often use metaphors to express their inner thoughts and feelings about themselves, or others, or their situations: 'I feel like a door mat'; 'My wife continues to build a wall between us'; 'It's like he's on another wavelength,' and so on.

Rather than paraphrase them, it is often helpful to integrate the client's metaphors into the counselling process (Wubbolding, 1991). For example, if the client says, 'I feel down in the dumps a lot of the time,' consider employing such questions as: 'What's it like being in the dumps?', 'What do you see when you look around?', or 'Do you want to get yourself out of the dumps?'

Listening and responding on this level helps counsellors empathize with their client and conveys to them that they are being understood. Clients may even feel an added sense of control and feel that their problems are more manageable. Witmer (1985) describes three purposes to such figures of speech: 'To give us greater understanding of what is already known; to provide us with greater insight into the unknown; and to enable us to express that which has aesthetic and emotional intensity.'

Wubbolding (1986; 1991) has written extensively on the use of metaphors and also paradox in the practice of Reality Therapy, and these two aspects are expanded upon in Chapter 10 of this book.

I *Listen for Themes*

In Reality Therapy the counsellor does not merely listen to feelings and reflect them back to the client, but additionally listens for, clarifies and reflects back the client's themes. For instance, the counsellor may discover that one theme of the client's depression is that they get depressed mainly in the evenings. Or the theme may be that the client most frequently generates anger when they perceive there are too many decisions to make. In group counselling, the counsellor can help to establish a trusting atmosphere by tying together the wants and/or perceptions of the group. The themes are then clarified by such statements as, 'Each member of this group seems to want to have a greater sense of inner control in one or more areas of their lives.'

Although listening for themes is not unique to Reality Therapy, it is nevertheless one of the foundational elements upon which the procedures that lead to change can be more effectively implemented.

J Summarize and Focus

Rather than just paraphrasing everything stated by the client, the skilful Reality Therapist focuses on themes and issues which pertain to the client's perceptions, wants and behavioural choices. An example of such a summary might be, 'Now, you think that other people see you as being cold and stand-offish; and you want to be popular and have more friends; but you also say that you enjoy being independent and doing your own thing.'

Other summaries might be limited to strength-building behaviours; that is, behaviours that resulted in effective control, behaviours that helped, or value judgements about what behaviours might be more effective in the future.

Summarizing in the manner described points to the need for focusing, and Reality Therapy is most certainly a very 'focused' method of counselling. By 'focusing' we mean putting the emphasis on one or more points, a theme, a critical idea, or wants, or unfulfilled needs, or a specific day in the life of the client, or what the client can realistically achieve, and so on. This is done with empathy as well as skill, as it may well be that the client is not 'ready' to focus on certain issues, perhaps during the first one or two counselling sessions, and needs time to express their concerns and feelings. However, the skilled Reality Therapist will look for the first appropriate opportunity to help the client put focus on key issues, wants, themes, behaviours and so on, and this will be a practice maintained throughout the counselling process.

K *Allow or Impose Consequences*

In some settings, such as hospitals, schools or probation facilities, staff members structure the therapeutic environment in such a way that clients experience the full range of consequences of their actions. Although consequences may be useful, no Reality Therapy programme should be established which has consequences as a cornerstone. They can easily be used or misconstrued as threats or punishments, resulting in 'boss management' (Glasser, 1994) or 'pop behaviourism' (Kohn, 1993a).

'Allowing consequences' means that one action flows from another. To fail to study in school has the consequence of failing the exam; consistently overeating has the consequence of putting on weight. Sometimes allowing consequences to ensue, rather than trying to protect or 'save' the client from experiencing the outcome or their own actions, can be more therapeutic and helpful, perhaps helping to raise the clients' awareness of responsibility and of the fact that behaviours have consequences. However, allowing consequences in such a way presupposes that the consequences are likely to be reasonable and most certainly not potentially harmful to the client or others.

Some settings, of course, require staff to 'impose' consequences and this seems particularly appropriate when anarchy or harm (to self or others) might otherwise be an outcome of irresponsible behaviour. Such settings would include addiction treatment centres, group homes and probationary facilities. Such imposition of consequences is not antithetical to the practice of Reality Therapy provided that it is imposed non-punitively; that is, without anger or exploitation. 'It is a simple matter of fact that a behaviour results in consequence' (Wubbolding, 1988).

L *Allow Silence*

Occasional pauses or periods of silence can provide the client with opportunities to reflect, gather their thoughts, clarify their wants and perceptions, gain insights and begin to formulate plans. Breaking this 'grand silence' can often destroy a very productive train of thought, so counsellors should quell the urge to break every silence.

Additionally, it can be useful at times to allow the client to take the lead after a period of silence, thereby taking some responsibility for the direction of the session as well as their total behaviours. Moreover, silence can prevent the counsellor from saying more than is necessary. It has been said that silence can sometimes be misinterpreted, but is never misquoted!

M *Show Empathy*

Many of the skills described here are techniques which can also enable the counsellor to communicate to the client that they are striving to appreciate and understand the client's point of view: to see it *as if you were in their shoes*, so to speak.

Establishing an atmosphere conducive to clear communication, personal expression and positive growth requires empathy on the part of the counsellor, and Reality Therapy is no different from the majority of theories in this respect.

N *Be Ethical*

All counsellors must know and practise the various codes of professional ethics, and Reality Therapists are, of course, no exception to this requirement. Ethical norms include professional disclosure, informed consent, and the avoidance of dual relationships (Wubbolding, 1986; 1993).

O *Create Anticipation and Communicate Hope*

Creating anticipation and communicating hope is something that relates very readily to other guidelines suggested, such as 'always be determined and enthusiastic' and 'never give up' (in believing that the client can build a better today and tomorrow).

Such *messages* of positive anticipation are conveyed to the client, not just in words, but more often (and very subtly) via the very manner, attitude and body language of the Reality Therapist. In such a way clients learn that the therapist has faith that they *can* change and, moreover, that something good or better can happen in their lives if they are willing to work at it.

P, Q and R: *Practise Lead Management, Discuss Quality and Increase Choices*

As previously stated, the 'Cycle of Counselling' also pertains to managing, supervising and coaching people (as the title in Figure 1 conveys), whether the setting be a school, workplace, hospital, agency (including a counselling agency) or anywhere else. Appropriate and skilful use of the 'do's' and 'don'ts' is as valuable to managing people effectively as it is to counselling.

Lead Management is the exact opposite of 'boss management' (Glasser, 1994) wherein the attitude of the 'boss' is mostly authoritarian and coercive. The 'boss' has the 'it's my way or the highway' approach in dealing with people. By contrast, the lead manager seeks to encourage and persuade, rather than use threats or coercion, supports democracy in respect of such things as the establishment of rules and working procedures, and encourages participation, particularly so with regard to *discussions about quality*, the 'moving target' (Deming, 1984) which all are encouraged to create and work towards.

To enhance such creation, the intention of the lead manager is to *increase choices*, and to listen and to respect others' opinions and ideas, rather than adopting the more rigid and dogmatic approach of the 'boss manager'.

Although these three 'do's' obviously pertain more readily to 'managing' than to counselling, they do nevertheless have a bearing on the counselling role, and counsellors should be aware that it is most certainly possible for them to impart (a 'boss-like') authoritarian or 'controlling' persona to their clients. Equally, they may, inadvertently perhaps, discourage clients from exploring their 'quality world pictures' (their wants), and, further, may even restrict the opportunities for clients to explore alternative 'choices' and behaviours in dealing with their problems.

Without doubt such 'controlling' behaviours by counsellors do exist, albeit in most cases unintentionally, and therefore counsellors would do well to consistently evaluate their own behaviours and agendas, as part of their own supervision and professional practice.

Conclusion

As previously mentioned, these guidelines need to be implemented by the counsellor or 'helper', not as rigid 'must do's' but appropriately and occasionally, based on considerations of the clients' emotional, mental, physical and spiritual condition and the particular counselling setting.

The following chapter provides some guidelines for *what to avoid* in trying to create a trusting counselling relationship.

CHAPTER 4

Creating the
Counselling Relationship (II)

The 'don'ts'

Having already provided some extensive guidelines for trying to create a warm, empathic and trusting counselling relationship (the 'do's'), it is also important to beware of some pitfalls (the 'don'ts'). Again, we refer you to Figure 1 on page 16.

As with the 'do's', awareness of the following guidelines extends beyond the counselling relationship to the many other areas where Choice Theory and Reality Therapy ideas are applicable: in schools, hospitals, criminal justice agencies, in parenting, coaching, supervising and managing people. Indeed, the ideas pertain to virtually every kind of situation where people want and need to relate effectively with others.

A *Don't Argue*

Although counsellors in private practice would be less inclined to get into arguments with their clients over principles or the rights and wrongs of behaviour and so on, nevertheless it does happen and when it does (whatever the setting) it invariably affects the relationship adversely, whether it be in the short or longer term.

The worst kind of arguments are the power struggles that emerge from time to time, whereby someone 'wins' and someone 'loses', the 'winner' being the one who can convince the other person that 'I've got it right and you've got it wrong.' Actually, with regard to building and maintaining good relationships, nobody wins. Both are losers. Therefore it serves no purpose to succumb to a power struggle over the rights and wrongs of rules, or behaviours, or of who started the fight, why a marriage is failing, or why the client has taken drugs, and so on and so forth. However, this does not mean that we are suggesting that the counsellor (or parent, teacher, manager and so on) should *agree* with the other party, but rather it is more effective to allow the potential argument to dissipate by saying such things as, 'Well, I see it differently', or 'They're the rules that exist at the moment', or 'Well, at least we agree that we see things differently!' And so on. Perhaps the best analogy for avoiding arguing comes from Dreikurs (1972) who uses the phrase, 'Take the sail out of their wind.' If the counsellor drops their sail (by not arguing) there is nothing to blow against, and the wind dissipates.

B *Don't Boss Manage*

'Boss managing' is the opposite of 'lead managing', which was suggested as one of the 'do's' for creating more effective relationships. The 'boss manager' exemplifies what can be referred to as 'sunshine management', as in 'Listen, sunshine, either you do what you're told or you're out!' The boss manager's motto is 'I'm in charge!'

Although this is an issue that fits more with management and supervision (in business, schools, probation or agencies, and so on) than it does with counselling, it does highlight an alienating attitude of 'external control psychology' (Glasser, 1998) that would be better discarded in virtually all human interactions.

C *Don't Criticize or Coerce*

Finding fault and telling someone what they 'should have done' creates a toxic atmosphere. Everyone chooses behaviours which they perceive to be the best choices for them at the given time. It is useless to criticize a person's best effort to satisfy their needs. Although counsellors are less inclined to resort to such behaviour, some can ultimately slip into this approach.

As Glasser has stated many times in his books and in his teaching (Glasser, 1984; 1994), criticism in any form – whether it be a comment, or a gesture, tone of voice, a look of disgust or disdain, or even the withholding of co-operation – only serves to drive people apart. Indeed the phrase 'constructive criticism' is most certainly a contradiction in terms.

Coercion implies using excessive pressure to elicit a behaviour from another person as well as using punishment when the behaviour is not chosen. The result of coercion is usually sloppy work, procrastination and even creative avoidance.

D *Don't Demean*

This means being sensitive to and avoiding any comments or gestures that could be interpreted as being demeaning or belittling in any way. This is particularly so with regard to efforts made by the client; each person's effort, even a (seemingly) feeble effort can appear to him/her to have a positive value.

The helper needs to genuinely feel, express and communicate a positive regard for the client.

E *Don't Encourage Excuses*

Parents, teachers, managers, probation staff and a high percentage of counsellors (trained in theories other than Reality Therapy) expend a great deal of time and energy trying to determine the underlying reasons for other people's unproductive, negative, destructive, upsetting or 'failure' behaviours. Invariably, this is attempted by asking, in one form or another, the relatively useless question, *'Why?'* Examples are 'Why were you late?', 'Why were you fighting?', 'Why did you fail the exam?', 'Why are you depressed?', 'Why did you drink too much?', 'Why did you eat the whole pie?', 'Why do you gamble so much?'

Repeatedly asking 'why' questions when people 'mess up' or 'fail' in some way invariably encourages the disclosure of *excuses*, in which control is attributed to outside forces: 'The reason why I was fighting was that he hit me first'; 'I failed the exam because the teacher was inadequate'; 'I drank too much because of pressure at work'; 'I gamble too much because I have an unresolved unconscious conflict'; and so on. It is rare (although not unheard of) for the person to say, 'I failed the exam because I didn't study enough'; 'I chose to drink myself unconscious' or 'I was late for work because I failed to plan adequately.' Merely asking the question 'why' when people mess up is often perceived of as a criticism, and the person immediately feels on the defensive, needing to come up with reasons or excuses in order to justify their ('failure') behaviour. Should the 'helper' (counsellor, parent, teacher, and so on) disagree with the excuse, the conversation can quickly deteriorate into an argument and a power struggle. Progress is thwarted and relationships become strained.

In understanding Choice Theory, the Reality Therapist understands the reasons behind all human behaviour and consequently there is little reason to ask, 'why' when people fail. All behaviour is an attempt to meet our specific wants and universal human needs, and people do the best they can do at the time they do it. Should the outcome of their behaviour be 'unsuccessful' or 'ineffective' in some way, they may change their mind about the appropriateness of their choices. Nevertheless, when the behaviour was executed it seemed like the best thing to do to fulfil their wants and needs. That is 'why' they did what they did!

Additionally, the willing acceptance of such excuses conveys an implicit message: 'You are not responsible for your behaviour and you can be excused and can get off the hook, so to speak, because you are powerless and cannot make any change in your life.' This is the reverse of the desirable message: 'You are strong and in control of your own behaviours. You can change you life; you can make a better plan' (Wubbolding, 1988).

So, rather than ask the 'why' question when it is anticipated that a barrage of excuses will follow, a more productive approach would be to ask 'evaluation' questions (to be fully explained in the next chapter) on the theme of 'Did it help or did it hurt?'; 'Did drinking yourself unconscious really help you deal with the pressure at work?'; 'Did it help enough?'; 'Do you think your manager regards your lateness as a positive or a negative, as far as your career goes?'; and so on.

Lastly, as alluded to several times already, the 'why' question is one that should be avoided only when people 'mess up' or fail and the counsellor anticipates that excuses will follow. It is, of course valuable to ask a technical 'why', an intellectual 'why', or to find out why a person succeeded. The essence is to avoid asking for irresponsible excuses.

F Don't Instil Fear

This guideline is really one that is more applicable to teachers, managers and parents than it is to counsellors. Indeed, most counsellors recognize that inducing fear is ineffective and does not increase perceptions of self-worth. Fear prevents learning and effective decision making, generates less than optimum performance, destroys relationships and impedes the effective fulfilment of 'quality worlds'.

G Don't Give Up Easily

This is certainly easier said than done. It is easy to give up with clients who are resistant, uncooperative, passive, apathetic, reluctant or hostile, or who relapse yet again. For the less experienced counsellor, there can be a temptation either to abandon the client or to abandon the theory when they discover that some clients are not helped instantly. Neither move is appropriate. The use of Reality Therapy is not an event. It is a process that requires time, effort, skill and repeated interventions (Wubbolding, 1994).

Summary

It is important to emphasize once again that the 'do's' and the 'don'ts' are suggested guidelines and not rigid 'must do's', to create a fair, firm, friendly and, most essentially, *trusting* counselling relationship. It should also again be stressed that many of the guidelines need to be employed appropriately and sparingly which, of course, brings into consideration the experience and skill of the counsellor. Additionally, it will be apparent to the reader that these guidelines extend beyond the sole criteria of generating an atmosphere conducive to positive change and, indeed, that some of them constitute techniques and approaches within their own right. These 'do's' and 'don'ts' are not only presented for counsellors to use in their therapy; many are also useful to teach directly to clients for use in their families, offices, classrooms and, indeed, in almost every human interaction.

Consultation, Follow-up and Continuing Education

These three additional guidelines, placed between the 'do's' and the 'don'ts' in Figure 1, are essential elements which are implemented outside the counselling session.

The *consultation* we refer to here includes the supervision which all counsellors are required to undertake according to their professional association's code of ethics. Obviously, the person who provides such supervision does not necessarily have to be a Reality Therapist but, of course, difficulties could arise if one's supervisor was unfamiliar with the principles of Reality Therapy or was opposed to such a cognitive–behavioural approach. We would also encourage consultation with one or more other Reality Therapists from time to time. Cases can be role-played or simply discussed, for, no matter how well a person practises Reality Therapy, there is always room for improvement. Such occasional consultation should apply to all who practise Reality Therapy, whether in agencies, schools, probation, social work, health care, addictions treatment, business and industry, or elsewhere.

Follow-up refers to later contact with the client: a telephone call, a return visit and so on. After termination of counselling it can be helpful, and it is usually appreciated by the client, if you make a follow-up 'phone call. The intention is to help reinforce any changes that the client has initiated, as well as being a gesture of care.

We regard *continuing education* to be essential for every counsellor, and indeed most agencies and counselling organizations require such professional development. It is important to stay abreast of developments in Reality Therapy, counselling, psychology, the helping professions and current issues.

Furthermore, consultation, follow-up and continuing education provide opportunities for evaluating one's professional effectiveness, and such self-evaluation is essential for all counsellors who commit themselves to the idea of providing quality service.

CHAPTER 5

The Procedures that Lead to Change: The 'WDEP System'

THE TRUST WHICH results from the establishment of a firm, fair and friendly environment provides a foundation for more directive interventions. The procedures described below constitute the essence of the delivery system. These components are not steps, but should be seen as a *systems approach*. They constitute a system and are thus interconnected. A counsellor can extract the appropriate element at a given moment for use in a specific situation. Secondly, they are applied to systems such as schools, families, agencies or businesses.

Each of the letters in the system represents a cluster of ideas and should be seen as a network of interconnected possibilities from which a therapist can choose.

'W' Discuss Wants and Perceptions

Users of Reality Therapy explore the quality worlds of clients. They ask especially what clients want to accomplish in the counselling process. The exploration of wants only *begins* with this question, however. Clients are also asked to describe what they want from other relevant areas of their lives, such as what they want from their families, partner, friends, job, supervisors, children, church, government and, most importantly, from themselves. In each area they can be asked what they will settle for, that is, what is the minimum that they believe will satisfy them. While these questions are easy to enumerate and can be summarized in a few brief sentences, still they are much more intricate and often more extensive in their implementation. A number of other questions are listed in the Wants Grid (Figure 2).

Asking clients what they want from themselves is a very useful intervention. This can take the form of a level of commitment: how much effort or energy they want to expend to live more effectively. Commitment can be expressed in degrees or levels.

Five Levels of Commitment
The five levels of commitment are discussed below.

1 *'I don't want help.' 'You have nothing to offer me.' 'Leave me alone.' 'Get off my back.' 'Get out of my life.'*
This commitment is the lowest and is really no commitment at all. Still, some clients express their degree of willingness to change in such words. These clients are often spouses, teenagers or probationers who feel coerced into counselling and have no immediate desire or want to change. They believe others are treating them unfairly and that it is the others who have the problem. The helper thus faces the challenge to provide convincing proof that it is in the best interest of the client to make a change.

2 *'I want the outcome, but not the effort.' 'I'd like to lose weight but I will not give up sweets or desserts.' 'I want to graduate but I do not care about studying.' 'I want my family to return and live with me but I'm not willing to give up drugs.' ' I want to stay out of prison but I'm not up to keeping the law.'*
Unlike the previous level of commitment, this level includes at least some desire or interest in a better life. Also the client rarely states this second level in such an explicit way. The words are unspoken or implied in other statements.

3 *'I'll try.' 'I might do it.' 'I could do that.' 'I'll probably do that tomorrow'. 'Maybe.'*
This middle level of commitment signifies a lukewarm promise to change behaviour. It represents a commitment developmentally higher than the first two but still will not accomplish much. Wubbolding (1991) described the airline pilot who announced, 'I will now try to land the plane.' Such an effort is praiseworthy but does not establish an

Fundamental generic question: What do you want?	1. What do I want that I am getting?	2. What do I want that I'm NOT getting?	3. How much do I want it?
A From my family			
B From my partner			
C From my children			
D From my friends			
E From my job			
F From my manager			
G From my subordinates			
H From the organization			
I From my co-workers			
J From my recreational activities			
K From myself			
L From my counsellor/teacher			

Figure 2 *Wants Grid*

4. How much effort or energy am I willing to exert to get what I want?		5. What will I settle for?	6. What am I getting that I don't want?	7. What are the priorities in what I want?	8. What is my level of commitment to categories A–L?	9. How do I perceive categories A–L?	10. What do I have to give up to get what I want?	11. What needs to be done regardless of whether or not I want to do it?

atmosphere comfortable enough for passengers to choose anxiety-free behaviours as the plane enters the final approach to its destination.

4 'I will do my best.'
Doing one's best is all anyone can do. But this statement frequently means that the person allows for failure. It is as though a caveat is issued that the person making the plan might indeed fail. Subsequently, someone can say, 'I did my best to be on time, but I just couldn't make it.' It is as though the therapist listens not only to the words of the client but to the *music* behind them.

5 'I will do whatever it takes.' 'I'm fully committed to the programme.' 'Nothing will stand in my way.'
When subsequent deeds match the words, this level has been achieved. Such a promise does not represent a fanatical or compulsively blind adherence to a plan or an idea. It merely implies a willingness to embark on a journey with resolve, vigour and perseverance.

The levels of commitment are useful in many settings. Reality Therapy has not only been applied to mental health counselling. It is widely used in schools (Glasser 1990; 1993) with regard to supervision and management (Wubbolding, 1996) and even to relationships (Glasser, 1995). Thus it is useful to ask such questions as the following:

- How much energy do we as a class want to put into learning history (science, literature and so on)?
- How hard do we as a group want to work at having a class which is enjoyable and where we can feel good about learning?
- What is our commitment to this job?
- How hard do you want to work at your relationship with your partner, spouse, children, parents and so on?

The reader is invited to develop more questions related to the levels of commitment.

1 _____
2 _____
3 _____
4 _____
5 _____

Users of Reality Therapy need to know that establishing the level of commitment is an initial step. It is maintained only when it is revisited occasionally and reinforced. Some clients experience a burst of energy when they enter counselling. Then there can be an ensuing plateau as well as a period of disillusionment in their efforts. Thus counsellors often need to treat the level of commitment as an underlying theme which permeates the process of therapy.

Explore Perceptions

Information is filtered through two levels of perception: the 'total knowledge filter' wherein the person recognizes people, data, things and ideas and gives them a label; and the higher level of perception or the 'valuing filter' which adds a positive or negative value to the perceptions.

A segment of a counselling session related to such exploration might be as follows. A woman, aged 35, discusses her marriage with a Reality Therapist. She has had an affair with another man after discovering that her husband has had an affair for five years. The dialogue reveals only the part of the discussion on perceptions. Here Th is the Therapist and S is Sue, the client.

Th: Sue, you told me you were disgusted with your husband. Describe what you see when you look at him, for example when he walks in the door after work.

S: I see a pig. An unfaithful, lying man who has misled me for years.

Th: You make many judgements about him.

S: Of course. I can't help it. He just seems to be like dirt.

Th: Is there anything he could do to help you change how you look at him?

S: He doesn't talk about it. I guess I might soften a little if he would talk about it.

Th: So you're not so fixed in your viewpoint that you absolutely won't change how you see him?

S: No. After all, I've been involved with someone, too.

Th: That brings up another question. How do you see your own role in all of this?

S: Well, I did some things because I was trying to get back at him.

Th: So when you look in the mirror what do you see – regardless of him and his actions?

S: Someone who is ashamed and guilty.

Th: So you see him as a pig and yourself as a …

S: As a sow.

Th: So you don't flatter either him or yourself.

S: All I see is darkness ahead for me.

Th: What about him?

S: The same.

Th: And the marriage?

S: I see it as going down the drain.

Th: Now I have a key question and I'd like you to think about it for a moment.

S: (Pauses) What is it?

Th: It's this. Do you want to see things differently?

S: (Pauses) Yes. I wish I could. And if I can't I'd like to end it and get on with my own career.

Th: Another important question, and it will sound simple, but it is central to anything you do in the future.

S: I'm ready.

Th: Is it helping you or hurting you to see things as you described them before?

S: It's definitely not accomplishing much.

Th: What impact do these viewpoints have on your marriage?

S: They certainly keep us apart.

Th: And you'd like to change them?

S: Yes, but I can't just forget or forgive him for what he's done.

Th: Of course not, but through this counselling you might be able to see other aspects of the relationship as you gain some experience in the post-affair period. You've indicated it's worth a try.

S: Yes, it is.

Th: No viewpoint will change just because you want it to. It will take a decision followed by action, by doing things. Only then will you change how you see yourself and how you see him.

S: Do you have any suggestions?

> *Th:* I'm glad you asked. In your opinion do you think I would have any suggestions?
>
> *S:* Judging from our other sessions I bet you have a lot of suggestions.
>
> *Th:* You are right on target. Are you interested in listening to them and considering them?
>
> *S:* Yes, that's why I'm here.

Clearly the client has explored her perceptions: how she sees herself, her marriage and her husband. The dialogue is intended to illustrate several questions focused on perceptions. A skilled user of Reality Therapy could expand on the areas which were merely touched on in this example.

The 'W' of the WDEP system provides the foundation for other interventions. And though it should not be seen as merely a first step, it sometimes precedes the other procedures. It is also an element which emerges throughout the counselling process.

'D' *Discuss Direction and Doing*

The 'D' implies that the therapist discusses the overall direction of the clients' lives as well as what they are doing. The discussion includes every aspect of their total behaviour: actions, cognition, emotions and physiology.

Direction
Questioning around direction usually is less time-consuming than explorations of specific actions, thinking, feelings and physiology. 'Where are you going, where are you headed if your current direction continues?' is an appropriate way to begin the discussion. So, when partners feel distant from one another, they are asked where they are headed: towards a better relationship or towards separation. The chemically dependent person can be asked, 'If your use of drugs continues to increase at the current rate, where will you be in five years?' The student who refuses to study or who makes little attempt to get along in the school can be asked, 'If you continue down this same pathway, where will you be at the end of the school year?'

This component can be connected with the previous 'W' also: 'Will you be where you want to be if you continue to choose this overall course?'

Doing
Helping clients consider their overall direction requires very little time, but reflecting on the specific elements of the total behaviour takes careful examination. Consider the following two scenarios and the implications of such introspection. In the first example, Cn is the counsellor and M is Mark, the client.

Cn: Tell me what you did yesterday.

M: I got up about 10am.

Cn: What did you do then?

M: I went to the bathroom.

Cn: Did you get cleaned up?

M: No, I just put on the bathrobe.

Cn: What then?

M: I went into the kitchen.

Cn: In your bathrobe without a shower?

M: Yes.

Cn: What then?

M: Just sat there at the kitchen table.

Cn: What were your thoughts as you sat there?

M: I was confused.

Cn: What went through your mind?

M: I was just numb.

Cn: That's how you felt. What were you thinking?

M: OK, I see. I was wondering if the effort was worth it.

Cn: Had some doubts about whether you wanted to live?

M: Yeah.

Cn: We can come back to that experience after a while. What did you do then?

M: Ate breakfast.

Cn: No kidding. You ate! What did you eat?

M: Five doughnuts and four cups of coffee.

Cn: What did you do then?

M: I watched TV.

Cn: How long?

M: Until lunch.

Cn: You ate lunch?

M: More doughnuts and about two more cups of coffee.

Cn: What did you feel during the morning?

M: I felt down – kinda depressed.

Cn: What thoughts went through your mind during this time?

M: I just wondered if all this is worth it.

Cn: We'll come back to that point again. What did you do after lunch?

M: Watched TV again.

Cn: Until what time?

M: I think it was about 4pm.

Cn: Mark, do you remember what you watched?

M: Not really. I didn't pay much attention. Sorta dozed off at times.

Cn: So you spent much of the day in your bathrobe in front of the TV except when you were eating doughnuts?

M: Yeah, I guess so.

It is obvious that Mark needs Reality Therapy immediately. But the point here is that the counsellor uncovered areas for counselling and future help merely by asking what he was doing: how he was spending his time, what he was thinking and how he felt at the time.

You are invited to expand the questioning by listing further possible questions related to 'direction' and 'doing' (actions, cognition, feelings and even physiology).

1 _____

2 _____

3 _____

4 _____

5 _____

6 _____

7 _____

8 _____

Below is another example. Please note the amount of information that is provided by even a cursory discussion of part of the 'D' actions. In this scenario, Cn is the counsellor and T is Terry, the client.

Cn: Terry, tell me about yesterday. What did you do in the sense of how you spent your time?

T: I got up about 6.15.

Cn: What then?

T: I clapped my hands and said out loud, 'It's a great day, full of opportunities.'

Cn: Did you believe that?

T: No, not at the time. But I believe it as the day unfolds. At the beginning of the day I'm as sleepy as anyone. But I feel more awake when I go through this brief ritual.

Cn: So you must have awakened pretty fast!

T: It works for me.

Cn: What then?

T: I took a shower and sang as I always do.

Cn: What thoughts did you have?

T: I truly believed it would be a good day. I look forward to going to work.

Cn: How did you feel?

T: Hopeful and mildly optimistic. I was beginning to wake up and think about the day.

Cn: What then?

T: Well, after getting cleaned up I did my stretching exercises. They take about 15 minutes.

Cn: What then?

T: Went to the kitchen and fixed my breakfast.

Cn: What did you have for breakfast?

T: Muesli, with a banana, and skim milk as well as orange juice to drink.

Cn: Sounds healthy.

T: Right! Then I sat in the chair and read part of a book I read every day.

Cn: What then?

> *T:*   Then I reviewed my 'to do list' to make sure that when I wrote it yesterday I put at the top the most important thing and at the bottom the least important item.
>
> *Cn:* What did you do then?
>
> *T:*   I went to work and started on the most important item first and then went through to the least important item.

This example, like the previous one, is intentionally exaggerated in order to make the point that a valuable short cut is available to counsellors. Examining at least part of a specific day in order to determine areas for counselling can speed up the process. Especially important are strengths or deficits in relationships with other people and activities which provide a sense of worth, enjoyment and independence.

'E' Self-Evaluation

The heart of Reality Therapy is the use of self-evaluation questions. No one changes any behaviour, actions, thoughts or feelings without first deciding that current behaviours are ineffective. Just as the driver of a car does not change direction if unaware that they have taken the wrong road, so too the driver of the *behavioural car* does not change direction without first concluding 'This choice of behaviour is not taking me where I want to go.'

In this crucial component of the WDEP process of Reality Therapy the client moves beyond the 'D'. Preceding self-evaluation is at least a statement about both the clients' current behaviour and their wants. They might have described them in a fairly non-judgemental way. At this juncture, however, the counsellor helps clients to judge, to evaluate the viability, appropriateness and effectiveness of the 'W' and the 'D'. Consequently:

The essential aspect of self-evaluation is a personal, inner judgement about behaviour or 'quality world' wants

It is not a guilt-ridden, compulsive, global, self-demeaning put-down characterized by self-contempt, but it does involve a willingness to take an honest look at one's own life. The types of self-evaluation which are most common include the following:

1   Is your overall direction taking you where you want to go? If you continue to go in your current direction, will you be helped or hindered? Will your life be enhanced or diminished by continuing down your current pathway? What is your current course of action accomplishing? What is its impact on others?

2   Is this specific action to your best advantage? Is it helping you or hurting you? When you did [name the action] did it help or hurt the people around you? Did it help to get the job done at work? What impact did it have on your family, job, friends, your future, your reputation and so on?

3   Is that specific action against any rules, written or unwritten? Was it within or outside the law? Even though you believed it was a good choice at the time, what do you think now as we sit here? Is it acceptable behaviour in this family, school or group to which you belong? Is it a behaviour you could justify publicly?

4   Is what you tell yourself really helping you? Will saying 'I can't' move you forwards or backwards? If you allow yourself to believe that the same choices will get you another result, will anything change? Does your current system of beliefs and assumptions support the way you would like to live in the future? What do you think about your self-talk? What do you think people who do not have this problem tell themselves?

5   Is what you want realistically attainable? Can you really get it all? Would it help you even a little to gain part of what you want? How would it help you? Can you settle for less than what you believe is ideal for you? For how long do you think you will be happy with what you can realistically get from ...? Does what you want from others encroach on their rights to have what they want? How is 'not caring' helping you to be free of external controls?

6   Is what you want genuinely good for you? At first glance, the desired object seems to be want and need satisfying but, after a

more careful examination, is your judgement the same? Like the dog that chases the car, what would you do if you 'caught the car?' What would you do with the desired object after you got it? What would you do differently if you had what you want?

7   Is your current level of commitment the highest you can make? If you do not do anything different, will you get closer to your [friend, partner and so on]? If you only want the outcome but change nothing over which you have control, what will be the result? How is 'trying' going to help you? If the airline pilot were to announce, 'I will try to land the plane,' are you going to feel completely confident, somewhat reassured, apprehensive or very worried? In other words, is your level of commitment the highest you can generate?

8   Is your current perception helpful or harmful? If you continue to see the world as you currently see it, are you going to feel better, do better or be better? In what way? Will you be happier in the future if your current viewpoints remain fixed? Will anyone else be helped or hurt? How? If you see only the negative side, the bleak side of life, will you feel any better? On the other hand, if you fail to see problems which reasonable people see, how will you be in a position to improve the situation?

9   If you have made a plan, is it really something you want to do or do you feel pressured to do something that deep down is undesirable? Does it fulfil the characteristics of an effective plan? Is it:
   ● simple: unambiguous and clear
   ● attainable: realistically doable
   ● measurable: answering the question 'When?'
   ● immediate: performed as soon as possible
   ● controlled by the planner: not dependent on others
   ● consistent: repetitive, if necessary
   ● committed to: firmly agreed to?
   How will you know if it is an effective plan after it is carried out?

Self-evaluation is a major contribution which Reality Therapy is able to provide to the profession of counselling and psychotherapy. Many methods help people formulate strategies and plans, but none is so explicit and clear-cut about the importance of this prerequisite for effective change.

Moreover, some people have special difficulty formulating inner self-evaluations. People raised in families characterized by turmoil, confusion or inconsistency incorporate pieces of data which are contradictory. Children praised and criticized for the same behaviour for a protracted period of time fail to develop the cognitive skill of discerning whether a specific behaviour is useful. Therefore, when they enter school, they need to be taught and counselled in a directive and unambiguous manner about behaviours which are congruent with the school setting and which produce harmonious relationships.

Similarly, individuals recovering from addictions very often have an underdeveloped skill in self-evaluation. Through the recovery process they can learn to relate to others in appropriate ways; that is, they, too, learn harmonious interpersonal skills.

In the 'Cycle of Counselling' (Wubbolding, 1996) (see Figure 1), *self-evaluation* is the keystone in the arch. All procedures and environmental elements converge on this central point.

'P' Formulate a Plan of Action

When William Glasser was an intern in a mental hospital, he was told by his supervisor, GL Harrington, 'Bill, when you don't know what to say to the patients, ask them "what's your plan?"'

The saying, 'to fail to plan is to plan to fail' applies to this procedure. As stated above, the plan should be simple, attainable, measurable, immediate, controlled by the planner, consistent and committed to.

Types of Plans

Plans fall into two categories: *linear* and *paradoxical*. The former is directly related to the problem. If someone is consistently late, the plan includes specific steps to be prompt. If the person is 'depressing', the plan is to take action steps to combat the depression. If someone will not talk to the therapist the plan is to ask them to speak.

On the other hand, linear planning does not always work. Some people rebel against direct plans. With a paradoxical plan, they can be encouraged, within ethical guidelines, to continue to choose the resistant behaviour. This technique is further explained in Chapter 10.

Another feature of the planning component is a strategy initiated by the counsellor. Clients can be taught Choice Theory and the WDEP delivery system. They can be taught that they choose their behaviours and that these choices are attempts to fulfil their 'quality world' and their five needs. Learning the WDEP system can facilitate effective control. When clients learn to define their wants and examine their behaviour as well as how to plan effectively, they have a methodology which can serve them in their families, in their workplaces and in all their relationships.

CHAPTER 6

Reality Therapy and Group Counselling

BECAUSE WE ARE social creatures, all human beings interact with others. Only the strictest hermit is truly a loner. And it is rare for such a person to seek counselling, especially in a group! For the most part people belong to families, work near to others and belong to trade groups, business groups or community groups. Whenever people gather and interrelate there will be at least some group process. People get to know each other, disclose information about themselves, move towards one another, enter into conflicts, resolve conflicts and finally accept or reject each other.

Some groups provide immediate ways for people to fulfil their needs and long-range ways to continue this fulfilment. If a person is lonely or isolated, a group can provide some immediate 'belonging' or a sense of involvement with people. Similarly, when someone feels out of control or is in trouble, a group experience can be valuable in that group members provide assistance in the search for a solution. Even an attempt to help can provide a sense of accomplishment. Groups can also provide fun for depressed people by helping them laugh. And finally when someone leaves a problem behind, a sense of liberation ensues.

Need fulfilment is central to a successful group. Thus, if the group is to be maintained and if it is to progress successfully through the stages described below, the leader must make conscious and specific efforts to ensure immediate need fulfilment through the enhancement of relationships.

Long-range need fulfilment is the ultimate goal of Reality Therapy groups. Participants are led to define their wants, clarify their perceptions, evaluate their behaviours and make plans related to their needs. Only then does need fulfilment result. The consequent carry-over outside the group meetings helps participants gain a sense of control, develop positive symptoms and feel better about the way they live.

Stages of Group Development

This chapter relies on the work of Corey (1995) who has provided an excellent model of group development. He has identified four stages of group process: (a) initial stage, (b) transition stage, (c) working stage, (d) consolidation and termination stage. Other writers have outlined the stages of group development in slightly different ways, but we have chosen to integrate Reality Therapy into Corey's description because his work is widely known and his stages are validated in our own experience.

This chapter includes a number of issues and tasks from each stage of group development. We have not attempted to utilize every issue or task described by Corey. Such an effort would be unnecessary. It seemed sufficient to choose several of the most important ones to illustrate how Reality Therapy interfaces with group development. At the end of the discussion of each stage, there is a chart which summarizes the tie-in between the stage and Reality Therapy. These charts represent extensions of the chart developed by Fahrney and Pettie (1987) but are limited to the integration of Reality Therapy with Corey's system.

To understand this tie-in it is useful to be aware of the components of Reality Therapy: 'environment' and 'procedures' (described in Chapter 5). The former implies creating a friendly, empathic atmosphere where people feel listened to, accepted and 'safe'. We summarize the procedures again here.

W = wants, perceptions and levels of commitment;

D = direction and doing: four aspects of total behaviour.;

E = evaluation: evaluation of total behaviours, of wants, of perceptions, of commitment, and of alternative behaviours and/or plans available.

P = planning for change.

These should be seen as a system, that is, the group counsellor selects what is useful at a given moment and implements it. There need not be a chronological, step-by-step sequence to the use of the components of the system.

The ideas contained in this chapter are applied specifically to group counselling or group therapy. Nevertheless, the overall model is applicable to other types of groups. Training seminars can be effectively based on stages of group development and integration of Reality Therapy (Wubbolding, 1987). Similarly, Palmer and Palmer (1983) seem to allow for group development when they speak about effective business and staff meetings. They describe the role of the leader and what they call 'meeting dynamics'. They state, 'By meeting dynamics, we are referring to the tone, character, and intent of discussion and interaction of meeting participants in session.' Though they speak of the process as if it were static, the stages of group development are quite applicable and the use of various elements of the WDEP system at different stages of meeting development can enhance business and staff meetings.

Initial Stage

Corey (1995) describes the first stage of group development as the stage at which *inclusion* and *identity* are dealt with. Participants wonder about their role in the group, whether they will be accepted and how they fit. They wonder how they should act, what is appropriate or inappropriate behaviour and what are the rules, both written and unwritten.

Members' behaviour is often that of watchful waiting. They expect someone else to get the group started. They remain in the background and, as Corey says, 'slip into a problem-solving and advice-giving stance with other members'. This is frequently due to anxiety for, if a 'quick fix' can be found, immediate relief occurs, without even the painful description of a problem, a want or an unmet need. And so a skilled leader quickly helps the participants to get beyond this anxiety.

Elsewhere Wubbolding (1987) has described several activities for counselling groups. It is assumed here that, if it is a counselling group, the leader has explained some basic rules such as that no illegal substances are allowed and that violence is not permitted. The leader will have explained and discussed the issues of confidentiality, informed consent and so on (Herlihy & Golden, 1996; Corey, Corey & Callanan, 1998; Ethical Standards for Group Counsellors, 1989).

Inclusion Activities

Participants are asked to explore their wants: what they want to get from the group experience, what possible benefits they see, how they feel about being in the group; what thoughts are going through their minds at the present time. Any or all of the above questions can be written. However, there is no need to overburden the participants with extensive written work. Extensive writing only serves to create more anxiety and resistance.

Participants then talk to each other in pairs or groups of three. They share their wants as much as is comfortable. No pressure is exerted on them to self-disclose. Each dyad or triad makes a group list on a flip chart-size sheet of paper and posts it for all to see.

Someone from each subgroup reads the list to the entire group. The leader then facilitates a discussion of the aggregate of 'published' expectations, thoughts and feelings of the participants. Questions for discussion include the following:

1   What are the common wants and expectations?
2   What are the common feelings and thoughts?
3   How much effort will it take to get the desired results from the group experience?
4   Why do you think that participants have some feelings (anxiety, fear and so on) as you enter this group?
5   Would anyone wish to comment on their 'published' or 'unpublished' wants, feelings or thoughts?

The leader should provide the following information and assurances:

1   All wants are legitimate. None should be seen as inappropriate.
2   Not all wants can be fulfilled 100 per cent. Some can be partially met.
3   All thoughts are legitimate. It is normal to have doubts about 'whether this group is for me'.

4   All feelings are normal. It is to be expected that some people will feel anxious, fearful and so on.

5   Benefits of group participation will vary among individuals.

6   Outcomes will depend on the energy and commitment the participants bring to the group.

7   There is no need to try to solve all problems at once. Nor is there a need to rush to solutions. Group progress will not happen suddenly, nor will individual progress necessarily be spectacular.

8   It is therefore acceptable to disclose as much as they see fit. They will not be manipulated into inappropriately choosing behaviours that do not coincide with values.

9   Maximum benefit is derived if participants are willing to take a risk, open themselves, listen to others and try behaviours different from those they have previously tried.

Some Reality Therapists prefer to use the activity 'Who am I?' early in the experience of the group, but not necessarily in the first session. It can be used either with a group whose members have used these categories to identify themselves previously or with a group whose members have not used them. They are asked to answer one question, 'Who am I?', without referring to any of the categories listed below:

Name	Place of Residence
Age	Family
Sex	Hobbies
Race	Professional Goals
Religion	Social Class
Credentials	Credit Rating
Occupation	Military Rank
Income	Physical Characteristics
Organisational Affiliation	Past Personal History
Political Views	

Participants are encouraged to use other information, other data or other aspects of their personality. It is not easy for some to strip away the usual designations and to look beneath the facade. Nevertheless, it involves only a slight risk on their part and so it can be used early in the initial stage of the group. It could also be used later after the group has passed on to other stages, and will then take on a deeper meaning for those who answer the question. The leader should suggest some types of information that can be used in the participants' self-descriptions:

Values	Ideals
Feelings	Attitudes
Wants	The person they would like to become
Needs	Spiritual goals
Need fulfilment	Relationships
Hopes and dreams	Degree of satisfaction with their
Frustrations	choices

The discussion of these data early in the group process helps the group in a number of ways. First, it develops a sense of inclusion. It is a structure, an exercise that quickly fosters a feeling of belonging. Second, it encourages the attitude that 'there is something for me in this group because the other people are both similar to me in some ways and different from me in other ways'. Third, it helps the participant to feel unique in the group and capable of making a contribution to the other members. Finally, it fosters interdependence, which helps participants feel a sense of belonging which underlies the issue of inclusion and identity. The immediate and often unspoken answer to their question, 'Who am I?' is 'I am someone who belongs in this group'.

The activities described above are intended to facilitate group process and to address the issues of inclusion and identity. Thus they should be seen as strategies, not as goals or outcomes. The leader uses them if it is judged that the group is ready for such activities.

Also the leader's task in a Reality Therapy group is to establish a friendly environment by helping people feel psychologically comfortable, answering questions, setting boundaries and so on (see Corey, 1995). More specific to the practice of Reality Therapy, the leader helps participants come to the belief that they are welcome and belong in this group. This is done by helping them explore their wants and goals: their reasons for being in the group.

It is appropriate, also, to teach some basic principles of Reality Therapy at this point. A suggestion is 'KiS': Keep it Simple. In the initial stage it is most effective if the needs alone are explained. The members are taught that when they are upset or have problems their inner needs are not being met. Each need can be explained, but it is ineffective at this early stage to stress the notion of 'internal control'. A perception that is widespread at this stage is that participants perceive their 'locus of control' as outside themselves. Thus someone describes a depression as caused by a divorce, a child on drugs, unemployment or a death in the family. An explanation about the reason for the person being depressed which is provided too soon is seen as a confrontation and a lack of empathy, with the result that the need for belonging is violated rather than enhanced. A discussion of how the participants perceive

STAGE 1: INITIAL STAGE

Issues, tasks	Need fulfilment	WDEP applications	Role of leader
1 Inclusion and identity	Belonging	Wants, Doing, Total Behaviour 4 aspects	Sets comfortable psychological atmosphere. Leads 'Who am I' discussion.
2 Goals	Belonging and power	Wants	Helps participants define what they want to get out of the group. Teaches four psychological needs.
3 Structuring	Power	Wants	Discusses informed consent. Explains rules and boundaries. Shares wants.

Source: Stages of Groups adapted from Corey (1995), *Theory and Practice of Group Counseling*, Brooks Cole Publishing Co, California.

their 'locus of control' is best brought into the open as part of the counselling. Only then are participants ready to hear the details of the theory. Awakening to the realization that behaviours (feelings) come from within us is a gradual process.

Transition Stage

Corey (1995) describes this stage as 'difficult' for the members. They must deal with anxiety, resistance and conflict. Yet, if they handle these issues, they develop a sense of trust and cohesion with each other and with the leaders. They had initially felt a sense of belonging (inclusion) but now have discovered that power needs are in evidence. They become marginally aware that, in order to benefit from the group, they will need both to take risks and to be committed to making uncomfortable efforts towards change. Such consciousness is accompanied by a sense of anxiety and fear of the unknown. This anxiety expresses itself by challenging the leader. Corey states that participants often confront the leaders by pointing out that they have encouraged the participants to self disclose aspects of themselves and yet they (the leaders) have been less than candid with the group. It has been our experience that even in classes on group process, students in some way symbolically expel the instructor from the class at this stage. It might be a challenge to the grading system, the content of the course or a demand that the instructor justify their competence to instruct. It makes very little difference how well the students know the professor or how many other classes they have had from them. The issue is one of process, not content.

Moreover, within the context of Reality Therapy, the participants in a group at this stage have progressed beyond the niceties of getting acquainted and have now discovered that real differences exist: the person whose sense of humour kept the group light is now seen as attempting to hold the group back; the silent one is seen not as shy, but as hiding from the group; the person who asks questions of others is now seen as nosy. Conflict results and is part of the process. For a group to mature, conflict must come to the surface.

The leader of the group at this stage helps group members recognize and express their feelings, and points out power struggles and resistive behaviours (Corey, 1995). Specific to the practice of Reality Therapy are several tools that address the above issues.

1 Teaching that there are levels of commitment which they can consider if they are to fulfil their wants as described earlier.

a *'I don't want to be here. This group has nothing to offer me.'* Even at this stage there may be some members who are at this low level of commitment. Reality Therapy is widely used in correctional settings where residents of institutions must attend group counselling sessions. For some resistance can be high even when other group members begin to express themselves and to deal with problems.

b *'I want the outcome but not the effort.'* It is useful to explain that a clear want is laudable. Yet, to achieve it, the group members need to move to a higher level of commitment.

c *'I'll try. I might. I could.'* This level is the beginning of behavioural change. The leader explains that when group members reach this level they are headed in a positive direction. This explanation need not be detailed. In fact it might even be merely an off-hand comment such as, 'You said you would 'try'. That seems to be a big step in the right direction.' This level and the next level of commitment are usually attained very gradually and become more explicitly expressed only in the working stage. Because there is still a sense of anxiety and conflictual behaviours at the transitional stage, the participants do not get to choose to elevate their commitment beyond 'I'll try'.

d *'I'll do my best.'* Although it is true that all one can do is one's best; this statement very often leaves the door open to possible failure. For example, someone might say, 'I'll do my best to be sociable', but have the qualifying thought of '... as long as other people are sociable towards me first', or 'as long as I feel like it', and so on.

Frequently it can be a case of 'It's not what you say but the way that you say it', as the song goes. Therefore, the counsellor should listen carefully for the music behind the words, so to speak, and if he or she is uncertain about the level of commitment expressed by the client, should explore further any such possible caveats or uncertainties the client may have about their commitment to change.

Such 'exploration' by the counsellor will invariably be accomplished more effectively by asking self-evaluation questions; as explained more comprehensively further on in this chapter.

e   *I'll do whatever it takes.'* The highest level of commitment often is the result of an evolutionary process, though occasionally members enter the group with this level of commitment. Others are more hesitant to work on their issues at this second stage and to make such a firm commitment.

The above levels of commitment are appropriately explained at this stage of group development unless the group is locked in conflict. Asking the members about their levels of commitment and internal obstacles to progress is a useful activity. This can be related to each level of wants in their list of priorities.

2   It can also be very helpful to teach that wants usually exist in an order of priority and that each want can be committed to in turn, thereby increasing the likelihood of success. Prioritizing wants appears to be easy. Nevertheless, many people such as addicted persons and their co-dependent family members frequently have major difficulties with this task. Achieving this skill might be a goal of some or all of the members of the group.

3   Using the Wants grid (see Figure 2) to help participants learn the wide range of wants that they can develop. Though not every issue surrounding every want can realistically be resolved in the group, participants are encouraged to put their wants in order of priority, to refine their original wants and to determine what can realistically be accomplished.

4   Pointing out that in the early stage of the group the need for belonging was most manifest. Now that power struggles have developed, the group is maturing and power needs are becoming evident. Thus the paradoxical technique of positive reframing what appears to some to be negative is useful at this stage.

5   Modelling the honest sharing of feelings about challenges to your role as leader, as well as providing assurances for those who feel anxious and helping group members recognize 'the ways in which they react defensively' (Corey, 1995).

The transitional stage involves a temptation to give up both on the part of the members and on that of the leader. But if the group deals successfully with the conflict they can progress to the working phase where their energy and efforts have deep and long-lasting rewards.

STAGE 2: TRANSITION STAGE

Issues, tasks	Need fulfilment	WDEP applications	Role of leader
1 Anxiety	Belonging, power	Environmental components	Listens empathically and reflectively to anxiety of members. Teaches there are priorities in wants system.
2 Conflict	Power	Wants, evaluation, reframing	Emphasizes that conflict is progress in that members are willing to speak their minds.
3 Control			Helps members clarify wants.
4 Resistance	Power	Paradoxical planning, reframing	Points out that resistance is normal and represents progress. Elicits at least 'I'll try' level of commitment.

Source: Stages of Groups adapted from Corey (1995), *Theory and Practice of Group Counseling*, Brooks Cole Publishing Co, California.

Working Stage

As in the passage from the initial stage to the transition stage there is no absolutely clear delineation, so too the group's entrance into the working phase is not marked by behaviours unique to it. Nevertheless, several elements can be described as most characteristic of the working stage of group development.

Having conflicted with each other during the transition stage by rejecting help offered by other members, and having challenged the legitimacy of the leader's role, the group members have now established the perception that they are able to work together. The leader has passed the 'competency test' and the group members come to the conclusion that the group as a whole, including the leader, possess skills, talents and ideas that are attractive and desired. This perceived ability to support and nurture the members is known as cohesion and is a need-fulfilling (belonging) quality that serves as the basis for interventions by the leader which lead to action planning by the members. Napier and Gershenfeld (1985) state, 'a cohesive group is one that members find meets their needs, or one in which they desire to remain for some other reason ... a highly cohesive work group might develop group pride and produce at a high level'. He cites Baird (1982) who reported that 'prior sharing between individuals produces greater cohesion and co-operation in later problem situations'.

Another issue which group members face is a higher level of commitment, which can take many forms. It can be a commitment to self-improvement or personal growth, to solving problems, or a commitment to the group itself. This commitment to personal change fulfils the need for power and achievement and the commitment to the group enhances belonging in all members.

Thus a co-dependent group member might decide to join al-anon or to stop attempting to change the spouse and to 'let go' of previous relentless efforts to control the chemically dependent spouse. In group counselling with married couples, one couple might reach a point of genuine interest in and desire to help another couple in the group. In some counselling groups, such as ex-offenders who are required to attend, this aspect of the working stage might be difficult to recognize. Still, it could take the form of a deeper willingness to make the effort to retain a job, to keep the rules of probation as well as a genuine desire and commitment not to revert to past destructive behaviours. Such groups conducted in halfway houses are characterized at this stage by altruistic behaviours that are sometimes quite remarkable. These choices increase the sense of inner control and competence (power).

Cognitive Restructuring

Corey (1995) describes a third characteristic of this stage as 'cognitive restructuring'. During this stage a change in thinking behaviours occurs and the members conduct an honest and sometimes searching and fearless inventory and evaluation of the effectiveness of their behaviour, the attainability of their wants, the helpfulness of their perceptions or world view and the depth of their commitment to change. From the point of view of Reality Therapy, such change in thinking should always be connected to and followed by action planning. Plans should be realistic, simple and revised at subsequent meetings. A married couple might decide that failure to spend time together is ineffective for maintaining a healthy marriage. They then plan to spend an hour each night doing something that is need satisfying to both. Ex-offenders in the halfway house might look inward and decide that continual complaints about the staff and avoiding responsibilities is a behaviour that is similar to the patterns which created trouble for them in the past. Thus residents might decide to be more conscientious in fulfilling responsibilities in the halfway house as well as controlling impulses in specific ways.

When clients help each other make plans they gain a sense of importance because their assistance is respected and accepted. When they are the receivers of help they feel an increase in belonging and power and they often cherish the attention and resulting surge in belonging.

Confrontation

In this stage participants confront each other about behaviour. In some groups they have been taught the WDEP system and are capable of asking each other evaluative questions about wants, perceptions and levels of commitment. On the other hand, the confrontation can take the form of 'you' messages: criticism, blame, anger and self-righteousness.

Such statements as 'We've all been working hard on our problems, so why don't you, Lee, work on yours too?' are often heard.

Leader's role
The role of the leader is to facilitate the interdependence of group members with a resulting increased cohesiveness through which members feel they 'belong' in this group. This is accomplished by helping them further define their wants in more personal terms than in the initial stage. They are asked what kind of persons they want to be, whether they (co-dependents) want to live their lives consumed by the behaviour of the chemically dependent spouse. Do they want to make a drastic turn in their lives and live a crime-free life style (ex-offenders)? Do they want to be proud of their spouses, of their marriage and of what they can bring to the relationship (married couples)?

The leader looks for commonality of wants which builds a sense of cohesion in the group. This is balanced with a feeling of diversity which allows individual members to see others as capable of helping them. Thus even diversity can be used to increase interdependence.

The leader also helps the members elevate their *levels of commitment*. If they were previously at the 'try' level, they are encouraged to evaluate this level and to restructure their thinking by evaluating their behaviour and so on. The leader links one member with another not only by asking each to evaluate their own respective behaviours and wants but also by asking one person to evaluate someone else's behaviour. Thus the leader asks one member of the co-dependents group, 'Fran, when Kelly threw the liquor down the drain did it help? What effect do you think it has on Kelly to do that?' It is important to note that this kind of evaluation is directed towards behaviours, not towards the persons themselves. Furthermore, even this kind of evaluation by member linking is not likely to be very successful until this third stage, when there is some degree of cohesion among group members. Expressing the leader's own opinions – sharing perceptions about effectiveness – is quite acceptable in Reality Therapy and often constitutes an additional healthy confrontation. If done in an artful way, the need for belonging is not only not damaged but, along with freedom, it is enhanced in that the person now feels accepted, recognized and even valued by the leader and group members in spite of weaknesses and occasional poor choices.

Leaders stress the importance of not only staying in the 'here and now' but of specific planning and life-style changes. Thus a smoking cessation group is aided with specific plans for substituting more effective behaviours and alternatives. Similarly a rehabilitation therapist helps patients evaluate such ineffective behaviours as failure to take medication or to get exercise. This is followed by specific tactical (short-range) and strategic (long-range) planning.

Plans should be characterized by qualities summarized in the following mnemonic: SAMIC3/P. Any plan should be:

Simple
Attainable
Measurable
Immediate
Consistent
Controlled by the planner (not an 'if' plan)
Committed to by the planner

The common denominator is that of perseverance. Neither the leader nor the client should fall victim to the advice of WC Fields, 'If at first you don't succeed, try once more, then give up. There's no sense making a damn fool of yourself.' Rather, the attitude to be communicated should be that of Thomas Edison, who tried 10,000 experiments before he found one that worked. Someone asked him how it felt to be right where he started from. He replied that he was not right where he started from: he was 10,000 steps ahead of where he had been previously, because he now knew 10,000 things that did not work! Such reframing by the leader allows group members to feel a sense of control, power and achievement.

The leader also uses paradoxical prescriptions besides linear plans. Thus the resistant participant can be restrained from making change. The obsessive participant in a mental health group could be encouraged to plan to return home x times to check the gas jets on the stove. Details of this technique are described elsewhere (Wubbolding, 1996). Such paradoxical techniques, always used with caution, are encouraged only within ethical guidelines.

In summary, the working stage is characterized by participants confronting themselves, sharing on a deep level and disclosing their wants, their 'out of balance scales', perceptions and so on. They also conduct a serious evaluation of their behaviours, wants and so on and,

STAGE 3: WORKING STAGE

Issues, tasks	Need fulfilment	WDEP applications	Role of leader
1 Cohesion	Belonging	Environment, wants evaluation	Identifies commonality of wants. Encourages feedback and assistance among members (evaluation).
2 Commitment to change	Power/ Achievement	Wants: Five levels of	Helps members to elevate their levels of commitment.
3 Cognitive restructuring	Power	Evaluation	Emphasizes members' evaluation of behaviour
4 Action, planning and implementation	Achievement/ Power	Reframing: linear and paradoxical plans	Assists members to reframe failure. Encourages action planning.
5 Confrontation	Belonging, freedom and independence	Doing, perception, evaluation	Shares perceptions. Teaches effective ways to confront without criticism. Emphasizes use of (E) Evaluation.

Source: Stages of Groups adapted from Corey (1995), *Theory and Practice of Group Counseling*, Brooks Cole Publishing Co, California.

finally, they formulate and carry out action plans within and outside the group sessions.

Consolidation and Termination Stage

In the final phase group members are often enthusiastic about having completed the group experience and having made changes, and at the same time they feel anxiety or even fear because the familiar support group will soon cease to exist and they sometimes express sadness at leaving the group. On occasion, some group members sabotage their own success: a member of a group at a halfway house for ex-offenders may choose to break a serious rule or even to violate probation in order to remain within the confines of the house and group and feel secure.

Anxiety and Fear

Generally, a more direct expression of anxiety is heard, such as, 'I don't know how I can maintain my new habits without the support of this group' or, simply, 'I'll miss all of you.' Sometimes plans are made to develop a mailing list to stay in touch. This type of follow-up is rarely sustained and can be seen as a reluctance to close the group. This hesitancy, anxiety and even fear of the future often accompanies a successful group because members have achieved a high level of need fulfilment (belonging, cohesion).

Unfinished Business

Another task, as described by Corey (1995), is that of completing unfinished business. To provide final feedback to each other and to put closure on the group experience provides a sense of completeness (power and achievement) for the members. An important part of this stage, and one contributing to the sense of completeness, is when members describe their progress and the changes they have made. Almost inevitably other group members provide observations that add to this sense of accomplishment.

Thus, in a group of married couples, when one pair describes how they now see each other's point of view more effectively and spend more time together, a group member might observe that they also seem to be able to listen to each other more empathically and to be less eager to 'diagnose each other's problems'. The co-dependent member might say that they have stopped trying to change the spouse's drinking behaviour, leading a group member to point out that this is a major step in the recovery of a co-dependent. An ex-offender might relate how happy they are to have held a job for several months without getting into trouble, and another member will add, 'When you first came to this programme, I thought you were cold and snooty. But I came to like you and I'm sorry you won't be here any more.' The opportunity to express progress and to hear additional feedback on unspoken successes is extremely need-fulfilling (belonging, power).

Future Map

A final task is that of carrying the learning further. The participants describe their progress and the changes they have made. They develop what we call a 'Future Map', strategies for maintaining change, adding to their resources, handling problems that will inevitably arise and dealing with relapses. In formulating a comprehensive strategy, and after learning the WDEP system of Reality Therapy, they will later be able to design specific tactical plans for dealing with various contingencies.

Work of the Leader

The efforts of the leader are aimed at allowing the group to discuss from a low level of perception, that is, without criticism, their feelings of sadness, fear, anxiety, hope for the future or pride in what they have accomplished. Such discussion is always linked to actions, especially specific plans, that is, their Future Maps. Support and validation of all feelings and positive plans at this time are important. Participants are encouraged to perceive their feelings as natural and normal, including fears and anxieties they may have about separation from members once the group terminates.

The leader also directly asks members to provide feedback to each other as a final gesture of friendship. The leader stresses that the comments made are most appropriately positive; no late 'bomb' should be dropped. The leader points out that now is the time to complete the unfinished business, not to uncover new issues that cannot be dealt with adequately.

The members are asked by the leader to summarize their progress. The leader who helps all individuals to participate in this process and recognizes that, even at this stage, some participants will be hesitant to 'brag' about themselves. With the help of the leader's direct questioning, the participants evaluate their progress. They describe how they have changed behaviour and they draw up a 'Future Map'. The married couple, for instance, who have stated that they now see each other's point of view and spend more time together conversing in non-critical ways are asked by the leader questions about the future.

1   How committed are you to continue these behaviours?
2   What problems do you see arising in the future?
3   What obstacles do you see to the continuance of your plans?
4   How will you deal with problems and obstacles?
5   Is there anything you need to start to do to deal more effectively with problems and obstacles?
6   How will you handle the urge to relapse or the fact of relapse?
7   What areas do you still need to work on?
8   What kind of support system will you attempt to build after this group's work has been completed?

Thus the members are encouraged to formulate ways to maintain their effective behaviours and to cope with the urge to choose the old, less effective or destructive alternatives.

In summary, the leader's work at this stage is to help the participants review their progress, say 'good-bye' to the group and plan for the future.

Conclusion

The stages of group development, described by Corey (1995), are quite applicable to Reality Therapy groups. The effective Reality Therapist is aware that need fulfilment should be facilitated at each stage and that various needs are more prominent at various stages of development. At times the Reality Therapist listens and supports, at other times the use of 'evaluation' – helping participants determine the effectiveness of behaviours, the attainability of wants, the depth of commitment, and congruency of perceptions – is used to challenge participants. The WDEP system used in groups is most effective when geared to the personal style of the counsellor: assertive, laid-back, more directive or less directive.

STAGE 4: CONSOLIDATION AND TERMINATION			
Issues, tasks	**Need fulfilment**	**WDEP applications**	**Role of leader**
1 Deal with feelings: sadness, fear, enthusiasm, confidence …	Belonging	Doing: Total behaviour, especially feeling behaviours	Provides opportunity for members to be supportive. Validates all feeling behaviours. Helps participants to perceive feelings as normal.
2 Completing unfinished business	Power and belonging	Immediate planning, communicating	Provides opportunity for members to give final feedback to each other. Helps members to summarize their progress.
3 Carrying the learning further	Enjoyment	Perception and future planning	Helps members to (E) evaluate their progress. Helps members to summarize their perceptions of the future. Assists the members to develop 'Future Map': overall plans to deal with contingencies. Assists members to identify areas to work on in future.

Source: Stages of Groups adapted from Corey (1995), *Theory and Practice of Group Counseling*, Brooks Cole Publishing Co, California.

CHAPTER 7

Application to Schools

R EALITY THERAPY STARTED in a mental hospital and a correctional institution. When Glasser was the only Reality Therapist, and shortly after the publication of *Reality Therapy* in 1965, he was asked to give lectures throughout North America. The warmest reception came from educators and they wanted him to apply his ideas to the classroom. In 1968, he wrote *Schools Without Failure*, which described how to use Reality Therapy in a classroom with large groups. But because the problems with the educational enterprise extend beyond the classroom to the very quality of student performance, the expectations of both teachers and the public, he later combined the work of Deming (1984) with Choice Theory and Reality Therapy.

Deming taught that a company and even a nation can prosper if it builds products and provides services which are of high quality. While this sounds self-evident at this point in history, it was not always obvious after the Second World War. At that time the Japanese were the first to operationalize his ideas on a widespread basis but they are now used worldwide. In merging Choice Theory and Reality Therapy with the principles of Deming, Glasser states that school discipline, truancy, lack of technological support and even finances are not major problems. Rather, they are symptoms. The fundamental issue is the quality of the educational offering. When the students are managed in a 'lead' style rather than a 'boss' style, and when they are taught a curriculum which is internally satisfying, the surface symptoms lessen significantly and often vanish.

A process for attaining a higher level of quality in organizations is now in place but is continually developing. At the present time there are some 200 schools in North America which are members of the Quality School Consortium and publicly state that, as a unit, they are using Choice Theory and Reality Therapy.

In July 1997, Glasser reformulated the process and the criteria for schools seeking to become Quality Schools as defined by their use of Choice Theory and Reality Therapy. The following is an edited document used by such schools and written by Glasser.

●　●　●　●　●

The Quality School Specialists Programme of The William Glasser Institute

Ten years of experience has taught us a great deal about how hard it is to create a Quality School. While many people are very interested in the concept, the path from that interest to a Quality School is far from clear. But what is now known is that this is a systemic change and all who are involved will see the value of moving from bossing teachers and students to leading them. To do this the following points are critical to the process and, of the following, number 1 is by far the most important.

1   This process has to be initiated and led, from the start, by the school principal who uses 'Lead Management' (see pp26 and 76) in all he or she does.

2   More than 50 per cent of the staff must be enthusiastically involved and willing to devote at least two years to this effort and they also must change over to 'Lead Management' in all they do.

3   As soon as there is interest, all who are involved need to read *Choice Theory: A New Psychology of Personal Freedom* (1998) as this theory is the core of the programme.

4   Beside *Choice Theory*, the staff should read Part One of *The Quality School*, all of *The Quality School Teacher* and the lead article by Dr Glasser in the April 1997 edition of

The Phi Delta Kappan entitled, 'A New Look at School Failure and School Success'.

5   Ideally, all parents should also read the book, *Choice Theory*.

Once a school has committed to these criteria and the staff and parents start to read the material, The William Glasser Institute will offer instructors to train the teachers in the 'Specialty of Quality School Teacher' and the administrator in the 'Specialty of Quality School Administrator'. This is described clearly in Chapter 10, 'Schooling, Education and Quality Schools', of the new book *Choice Theory*. After at least two years of work, if the administrator and ninety per cent of the teachers can demonstrate to each other and to their school community that they are competent in this 'Quality School Specialty', they will be awarded a 'Certificate of Competence' by the Institute. At that time, the school will be awarded 'The Quality School Flag' that all Quality Schools fly daily from their flagpole.

To begin the process, the head teachers of all involved schools must enrol in a four-day 'Quality School Head Teachers' Seminar' in which they will learn in detail what their role is in leading their school towards becoming a Quality School. If a district is involved, all principals in the district should be enrolled in this seminar. Prior to that seminar each principal should read the new book, 'Choice Theory', part one of 'The Quality School' and the article in the *Kappan* previously mentioned. This seminar will be led by instructors in The William Glasser Institute.

The Quality School Specialists Training Programme

Phase One, Learning the Ideas
In this phase, instructors from The William Glasser Institute who have experience in schools and in teaching the Quality School ideas will be assigned to the school and, at the preference of the school, will work until the training process is

complete. The school can change instructors and supplement instructors any time in the programme. The school need not commit itself beyond one year to the programme.

During this phase, the instructors, assisted by the head teacher, will meet with the whole faculty and/or any part of the faculty to make sure that they are completely familiar with the ideas in the books. The instructor will also demonstrate the use of these ideas in the classroom so that the teachers see how they may be applied. Teachers who have begun to use the ideas will be encouraged to assist. Questions will be answered and parental involvement will be urged. It is estimated that this phase will take one year.

Phase Two, the Practice Phase
In this phase (which some teachers who have learned the ideas will begin during Phase One), all the teachers should begin to practice these ideas in their classrooms with the instructors consulting and demonstrating as they do this. Teachers will be encouraged to implement the ideas as they see fit; there is no one way to do this. There needs to be a lot of discussion as problems arise, especially, as the teachers move to what we call TLC or Total Learning Competency. It is the job of the instructors to follow this process until the head teacher, teachers, students and parents all agree that they are ready for Phase Three.

Phase Three, the Demonstration and the Awarding of Certificates
This is a celebration over two days in which all that has been accomplished by the staff, students and parents will be demonstrated to the whole community. The following are the minimal criteria for a school becoming a Quality School.

1   All disciplinary problems, not incidents, will be eliminated in two years. A significant drop should occur in year one.
     Discipline issues are the most glaring symptoms of the unmet needs of the students. Antisocial behaviour is an attempt to fulfil the need for power. If a school is a

Quality School it facilitates the fulfilment of this need in ways that are appropriate. Thus students can relinquish destructive actions. Consequently the use of Reality Therapy principles and the Quality School effort is not a discipline programme. There will always be incidents which need to be dealt with. But in a Quality School discipline as a school-wide condition has vanished.

2   At the time the school becomes a Quality School, achievement scores on standardized assessment tests should be improved over what was achieved in the past.

One of the cornerstones of the work of W Edwards Deming is continuous improvement. No artist paints the perfect picture, no athlete plays a perfect game and no student body or school faculty is perfect in every way. There is always room for improvement. The Quality School demonstrates the ability to continually progress.

3   TLC, Total Learning Competency, means that grades below competence, or what is now a B, will be eliminated. Students will have to demonstrate competence to their teachers or to be designated teachers' assistants to get credit for the grades or courses. All 'schooling' will be eliminated and replaced by useful education.

Students are expected to be genuine achievers. Thus they are not given 'free passes'. The Quality School is not an easy school. Students work hard because the information is seen as need satisfying, interesting, and relevant to their lives ('useful'). This is the opposite of the rote memorisation of useless information, lessons imposed ruthlessly without consideration of students' quality worlds, and an atmosphere of injurious competition ('schooling').

4   All students will do some quality work each year – that is, work that is significantly beyond competence. All such

work will receive an A or higher grade. This criterion will give hard working students a chance to show that they can excel.

The criterion for quality work is primarily but not exclusively the inner and sometimes public self-evaluation by the student. They are taught various forms of self-evaluation as well as how to illustrate their accomplishments via portfolios, demonstrations, etc.

5   All staff and students will be taught to use Choice Theory in their lives and in their work in school. Parents will be encouraged to participate in study groups to become familiar with Choice Theory. A few of these groups will be led by teachers to start, but parent volunteers will be asked to take the groups over once they get started.

The goal is to involve the community in the practice of Reality Therapy and Choice Theory. We suggest that learning the WDEP system can be a useful tool in this process. The formulation is applicable to parenting, managing, teaching and all human interactions.

6   It will be obvious by the end of the first year that this is a joyful school.

A joyful school is a friendly place. People know each other, treat each other with respect and courtesy, have empathy for those who suffer, believe that human beings are essentially good, not evil, laugh together, and feel a sense of excitement about learning and school activities.

Quality is a moving target and the above criteria are not easily attained or maintained. In fact they are not achieved perfectly. But a school using Choice Theory and Reality Therapy demonstrates year-by-year progress.

●　　●　　●　　●　　●

Not a Pre-Wrapped Programme

It would be very comforting if there were a step-by-step process for becoming a Quality School. But the push–pull, hydraulic, automatic outcome, one-size-fits-all programme is not, nor can be, available. Each Quality School looks different from others and is unique. Each school is encouraged to develop its own way to teach the ideas to students and to develop its own curricular materials. While the ideas are universal, the delivery system needs to be tailor-made for each school.

With caution in mind, lower and middle schools are advised to use the materials developed by Carleen Glasser (Glasser, C 1996a; 1996b). There is value in using them as pre-planned lessons, but the real value is that they provide a starting point, a launching pad for teachers to use in developing their own lessons as well as their own ways to infuse the ideas into their required curriculum.

Lead Management

In addition to teaching the concepts of Choice Theory and Reality Therapy as a cornerstone of the Quality School, consider the superstructure of Lead Management. This is the opposite of boss management. The boss manager is dictatorial, manipulative and lives by the motto, 'It's my way or the highway.' The lead manager is democratic, straightforward and lives by the following principles:

1. Involve people in decisions which affect them directly and indirectly.
2. Listen to all viewpoints before decisions are made, not merely to pacify students or workers after decisions are made.
3. 'Walk the walk'. Don't merely 'Talk the talk'. Model the behaviour which is desired in others.
4. Help teachers and students to learn to assess themselves using the forms of self-evaluation described in this book.
5. Provide support as well as encouragement for the development of ideas and also when people show initiative. Express gratitude as often as possible.
6. Teach that the heart of quality is continuous improvement.
7. Emphasize that the classroom, and the entire building, needs to be seen as a friendly place – a place where teachers, staff and students

can fulfil their needs for survival, belonging, achievement, fun and freedom.

In summary, the lead manager knows and practices Choice Theory and the principles of Reality Therapy. If this is experienced for a protracted period of time both managers and those managed (students) begin to unleash their creativity in responsible and productive ways.

CHAPTER 8

Relationship Counselling

BECAUSE THE PRINCIPLES of Choice Theory and Reality Therapy are universal they apply to the most intimate of relationships, such as marriage and the family. All people have needs, quality worlds, behaviours made up of actions, cognition, emotions and physiology, as well as high- and low-level perceptions. A skilled user of Reality Therapy applies a three-step methodology to relationship counselling: *assessment*, *intervention* and *action*. The lines between these three components are not absolute but are fluid. For example, frequently the assessment stage is revisited when couples demonstrate resistance to change.

The therapist first assesses the desire on the part of the clients to stay together, to maintain the relationship and to enhance their intimacy. Their level of commitment both to the relationship itself and to the effort to improve is identified. Questions which save time and cut through the usual smoke screens sent up by troubled families include the following:

- Do you want me to be a marriage therapist or a divorce therapist?

- Do you want to keep the family together or is it time to break up, move apart and divide up your possessions? (Invariably the answer is that they want help staying together or at least they want to 'try counselling before taking the final step of divorce'. The counsellor can then help them formulate a commitment as to how hard they want to work at deepening their relationship.

- Do you want to exert a little effort or all your effort?

- How would your relationship be different if you were to be getting along better?

- Describe what you did differently when you were happier earlier in your marriage.

- What were your actions like then? Your thinking? Your feelings.

The answers to these questions serve as a basis for intervention. Reality Therapy applied to relationship counselling includes two major interventions: determination of the strength of the five needs (see below) and use of quality time as a foundation for closeness.

Intensity of Needs

Using the scale described by Glasser (1995) clients are asked individually to identify the intensity or strength of their own five basic needs. They then try to assess their partners' need strengths. The goal of this rating activity is to stimulate lengthy discussions about how the needs play out in their individual lives and in their mutual interactions. They might even involve others in their effort to assess their need strengths. Glasser states:

> If your marriage is less satisfying than you would like, I encourage you to do this for your own marriage with or without your mate. You might, just for practice, ask some friends whose parents you know and who know your parents to join you in constructing a need-strength profile of your parents and their parents to see if you agree on what you have constructed. Talk it over and do it for other couples you both know also. Exercises like these will help you learn to construct accurate need-strength profiles. (1995, p76)

The order in which the needs are evaluated is as follows:

	Low Need Strength				High Need Strength
Survival	1	2	3	4	5
Belonging	1	2	3	4	5
Power	1	2	3	4	5
Freedom	1	2	3	4	5
Fun	1	2	3	4	5

Glasser speculates that there are profiles which are more compatible than others.

Compatible Need Profiles
The high-intensity need for belonging in both people is probably conducive to a good relationship, but a high need for power in both partners could spell trouble. If both are risk takers or financially conservative (low score and high score, respectively, on survival) they are likely to be compatible. Similarly, if both have high or low scores on the freedom scale they could be compatible. The same is true for fun.

Incompatible Need Profiles
Glasser (1995) remarks:

> The profiles of you and your mate can show you where you may be seriously incompatible. You can use this warning to deal with differences in the strength of your needs before problems get out of hand. This takes strength and courage, and some couples, especially

early in marriage, may find this approach unromantic. But a bad marriage is more than unromantic – it is hell. (1995, p77)

In order to approach this activity it is useful to desensitize oneself to the possible anxiety involved in the process. Using figures from literature or television shows could provide a good start. Scarlett O'Hara would probably have a rating of 52542. She was high in survival and low in love. Her scores in power and freedom were much higher than her score in fun. Rhett Butler, on the other hand, would probably have a 25455 profile. As a risk taker he was below average in survival, high in love but below Scarlett in power. His needs for freedom and fun seemed to top the scale. With these two profiles their relationship was irreconcilable (Glasser, 1995).

It is important to recognize that these need profiles are not absolute. No hurried decisions should be made merely on the basis of these subjective ratings. The purpose of these exercises is to encourage the couples to begin to talk about their own motivation, their quality worlds, that is, what specifically satisfies their needs, how they see their partners, what compromises each person can reasonably make in the relationship, and specific plans for the future. The activities provide content for discussion and are especially useful for couples who have spent their valuable time bickering and disagreeing. For more well adjusted couples, dialogue about their needs, quality worlds and total behaviours provide opportunity for a better, happier relationship.

Quality Time
The other major intervention is called 'quality time' (which is referred to initially here and expanded upon on page 87). This phrase has come to sound trivial, in that many events and things use the word 'quality' as an adjective. But in Reality Therapy the phrase has a specific and technical meaning.

Many tensions emerge in the best of relationships such as marriage, friendship and those between parent and child. Problems seem to surface at levels A and B (see Figure 3). Traditional methods of therapy focus on the interactions of the family at these two levels. Family members are taught to communicate more effectively by using 'I messages' (eg, 'I often say things I later regret'; 'I often feel angry about …') rather than the potentially accusing 'You messages' (eg, 'You never show me respect'; 'You make me angry when you …'). They are also asked to develop ways to solve problems and to compromise. These methods are at times helpful but frequently only serve to make the relationship worse. The reason is that there are no commonalties or few overlaps in the partners' quality worlds, total behaviours or perceptions.

Consequently, it is often useful to help the clients build a foundation for better communication, problem solving and compromise. If partners are to achieve a higher level of intimacy there must be overlap in their quality worlds (wants), in their four

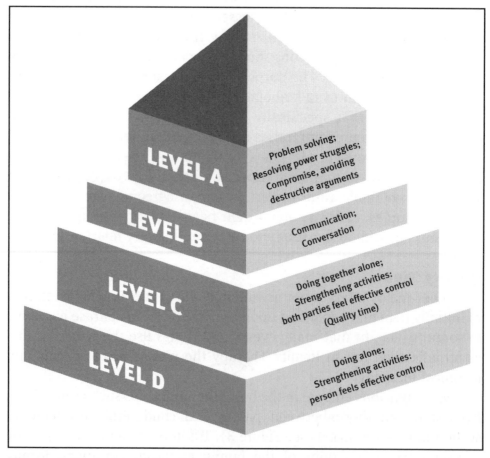

Figure 3 *Methods and Levels in Building Relationships*

components of behaviour and in the values they put on the information they receive from their external worlds.

The four levels of activity shown in figure 3 provide a way for couples to view their interactions in a developmental manner. If there is to be closeness in the relationship, all four levels need to be operational.

Level D: Activities Performed Alone

Samuel Johnson once remarked that, if people are to bring something home from their travels, they must take something with them. The same is true in relationships. When relationships are need-satisfying to both people beyond the acquaintanceship level both people bring a degree of autonomy, independence or self-worth based on what they do independently of the other person.

From the point of view of the Reality Therapist, the individual brings some ability to satisfy their needs. The person has at least some behaviours in the suitcase of behaviour that are separate from those used in the relationship. Having a job, a hobby, friends, social involvements, even a set of opinions or beliefs that individuals can claim as their own is very helpful in maintaining healthy relationships. Such autonomy prevents the intimacy-destroying behaviours seen in overdependence. Co-dependent spouses allow their lives to be dominated and ruled by the behaviours of the addicted person. In a way they derive their identity from the addict. Their choices are reactions to the all-consuming, inconsistent and even threatening behavioural patterns they see around them. In their embarrassment and shame, they abandon their outside interests, which leads to more loneliness, depression and anger. Through self-help groups such as Alcoholics Anonymous they can regain a sense of purpose, a sense of the universality of their plight, and intimacy. After gaining a sense of identity and a feeling of strength they can change their role in the relationship from co-dependence to more, though not complete, independence. They are ready to choose behaviours which at least render them capable of intimacy. Whether such closeness can be found in the marriage depends on levels C and D.

Not every relationship is characterized by such conditions. Still, a certain amount of autonomy enhances the relationship and precludes a less than healthy enmeshment. The following dialogue illustrates a conversation between a therapist and a client. Lucy, 43, wished to deal with her husband, Harry, who she discovered has been having an affair with a woman in another country. Here Th is the therapist and L is Lucy, the client.

Th: How can I help you?

L: My husband has been having an affair with someone in Spain where he frequently travels. (*She describes in detail how she learned about it. She talks about what he did.*)

Th: Tell me how this has affected you.

L: Well, he wants us to stay together. He says it's over between them. They've seen each other for years. I don't know how he can give her up. I've seen the letters and the pictures of them together. They seemed happy. He looked happier with her than he does with me.

Th: Tell me a little bit about how you have handled the situation.

L: He just refuses to talk to me about it except to say that it's over and we don't need to get into the details. He's very quiet around the house . . . just doesn't seem happy. He needs to be cheered up. He just mopes around when he's not working. Sometimes he brings work home and does some paper work. He's got a good job with the steel company and works a lot with the plants in Spain. I'm not sure what he does at work ...

Th: You said, 'I'm not sure what he does ...' That's the first time I've heard you say 'I'.

L: He's very secret about things. Always been that way. Even when he married me he didn't talk much about work.

Th: Here is another question. Do you want to stay together?

L: I'm not sure what he really wants to do. He says he wants us to stay together but he's only said that once or twice. He just doesn't say much.

Th: Let's try again. Do you want to stay together?

L: Well, I guess so.

Th: Is that a 'Yes'?

L: Yes.

Th: A firm 'Yes'?

L: A firm 'Yes'.

Th: I notice that when I ask about yourself, you switch to a discussion about him.

L: He's my husband, after all.

Th: Yes. But could you express your own viewpoint? I have other questions. But I'm asking you to express your own beliefs and opinions.

L: That's not easy.

Th: But would it hurt you to do so?

L: That's hard to answer ... I might have to ask ...

Th: (*Interrupting*) No. I want you to say unequivocally whether you think saying what you want, what you believe, or how you feel will hurt you. Keep in mind you're saying them only to me.

L: Well, I ... a ... a ... a ...

Th: Yes or no?

L: No. It won't hurt me.

Th: Now, I'm asking you about your want. Do you want to stay with your husband?

L: (*Pause*) Yes.

Th: Congratulations. Was it easy or hard to say that?

L: Very hard.

Th: I wonder why.

L: I'm not used to saying what I want.

Th: I understand that. I'd like to help you develop such a skill.

L: I think we need marriage counselling.

Th: That's terrific. You expressed your opinion and I agree.

L: You do?

Th: You seemed surprised that I agree.

L: I'm not used to anyone agreeing with me.

Th: I believe I can help you with some of these things, including marriage counselling. First, I think I should see you alone about 10 times.

L: I guess it would be all right with him.

Th: Is it all right with you?

L: Yes.

> *Th:* I would like to help you first so that, when we do the marriage counselling, it won't take as long.
>
> *L:* That would be OK.
>
> *Th:* You sounded firm when you said that.
>
> *L:* I did?
>
> *Th:* Yes. And I'd like to help you express how you feel, what you think, what you want and so on. Would that be something you'd like?
>
> *L:* Yes. You know, he does say that I have low self-esteem.
>
> *Th:* You can give any name to it. But I believe that, after we work on a few of these things, you'll feel better and stronger ... maybe more self-confident. Then the marriage counselling will work better.
>
> *L:* Sounds good.
>
> *Th:* See you next week same time?
>
> *L:* Yes.

In this situation Lucy was unable to fulfil any of her needs satisfactorily. Deficits were evident in belonging, power or achievement (self-esteem), fun and freedom or independence. The therapist chose to help her with self-esteem (power) and independence or freedom. The strategy of seeing her alone for a while was based on the judgement that marriage counselling might be less effective until she was able to make at least some choices on her own which would be designed to help her feel better about herself. Then she would be more suitable for marriage counselling. In other words, she would have something to bring to the therapy. If she was to gain anything from the journey of therapy and the journey of the relationship with her husband, she would need to bring something, at least a modicum of accomplishment and independence.

From a different perspective, enhancing the relationship can serve as an effective antidote to domestic violence. Jennings (1991) found that three approaches can be helpful: the unilateral emphasis that full responsibility be taken by the male and that he make the major number of changes; the bilateral approach where both spouses are expected to change, but treatment is conducted separately; and the dyadic approach, which focuses on the couple's interaction and on their work towards a common goal. Each of these, from a Reality Therapy standpoint, implies that the parties involved decide that they want a better relationship, examine the effectiveness of their behaviour and make more effective plans. This could involve examining the strength of their needs as well as their commitment to regular quality time.

Level C: Activities Performed Together: Quality Time

In formulating the principles of Choice Theory and Reality Therapy, a conscious effort has been made to use words which are easily understood by most people. There is some, but not much, esoteric language. Though the phrase 'quality time' has become in some ways a worn out phrase overused in the media, it can be a useful idea as understood by couples wishing to achieve more intimacy in their relationships.

As shown in Figure 3, Level C summarizes quality time which is one of the foundations upon which is built better communication and the skill of resolving conflict. Quality time implies more than being together. Many people can be in the same place, do the same thing and even feel the same way about something. Thousands of people attend sporting events and have virtually no relationship with each other before, during or after the event. And so, for an activity to be called quality time and thus be a building block for intimacy, several characteristics must be present.

1 Takes Effort

Passive activities such as watching television or sleeping in the same bed do not qualify. Even eating or driving together are less helpful than playing a game together, or having a hobby or an interest that is satisfying to both parties.

The average television set is turned on for many hours each day. It is not surprising that people can live under the same roof and feel alienated, lonely, anxious and even panicky. During this time there is little strength and even less intimacy built into the relationship. In fact, behaviours antagonistic to intimacy are often inserted into the mind of the viewer. It is sufficient to say that the average seventeen-year-old will have seen thousands of murders and acts of violence, countless arguments, endless aggression as well as explicit, casual sex and an untold number of people in states of continuous crisis. The lessons learned can include the following: violence is glamorous, promiscuity is to be valued, problems are solved by anger and rage and, finally, people interact best by demeaning and belittling each other. The popularity of educational and uplifting programmes has yet to equal, much less exceed, that of the aforementioned kind.

2 *Value for Each Person*
The activity is seen as mutually positive. Going to a political fundraiser might be a lifetime high point for one person but a total bore for another. If grocery shopping is enjoyable to both it can be used to build the relationship. But if one person is annoyed and sees it, at most, as a necessary and burdensome task, the 'togetherness' is diminished. On the other hand, if it is fun for both people, intimacy is enhanced. If the activity is agonizing, irritating, uncomfortable or even performed exclusively as a painfully altruistic behaviour, it will not improve the relationship.

The exact nature of the activity is thus negotiated. The grocery shopping trip is a relationship-building activity for some people. For others it provides more than an ample supply of tension and aggravation.

3 *Includes Enjoyability or Fun*
This component is the reverse of numbers 8 and 9 below. The activity is something which builds a storehouse of positive perceptions or memories. Picnics, exercise, even house cleaning are enjoyable to some. But if the activity is repulsive it will diminish the relationship. When the necessary unpleasant activities are performed, they need to be balanced by enjoyable discussions, joke telling, hobbies, or some agreed upon fun.

4 *Performed for Limited Time*
The activity is carried out for short periods. Long periods are not recommended, especially if there is tension in the relationship: 10 or 15 minutes a day, or even less, can suffice. The actual time depends on the inclinations of the couple – the decision is based on the amount of already existing strength in the relationship – but 10 to 15 minutes a

day is often realistic and attainable. It does not require a major revolution in scheduling. The outcome of this time together provides a solid basis for nurturing a relationship. It would be a mistake to minimize the value of these few moments spent together. The more connectedness existing between the two people the longer the time can be; if the couple has a high degree of overlap in their wants, behaviour and perceptions the time can be longer.

5 *Requires Repetition*

For the time to be useful, the activity needs to be repeated regularly. Just as one 30-minute period of running or jogging does not produce an accomplished athlete, so too one brief period of quality time or an occasional effort does not result in a solution to the problem. This tool is not a quick fix. A solid basis for a happy relationship is built on activities performed over and over again. The results are often seen after weeks and even months of repeated decisions, planning and follow-through on this joint effort.

6 *Involves Mutual Awareness*

The activity is such that each person is aware of the other's presence. Thus watching television is again disqualified, or at least rendered less effective than a tennis game or a brisk walk. Driving and riding in a car is barely within the rubric of quality time. Even sleeping together is questionable, for at such times of unconscious proximity the partners are oblivious to each other's presence.

7 *Discussion of 'Safe Topics'*

Strengthening and deepening intimacy occurs when couples spend time together talking not only about intense subjects but about topics which correspond to the lower level of perception. It is evident that difficult topics and painful issues need to be deal with. Still it is useful to have some time set aside when light conversation is the focus. Wubbolding (1988) describes a couple whose son was hit by a car. The family talked about the pain, the regrets and the 'if only's'. The counsellor asked them if the continuous repetition of such discussions helped them feel better. They agreed that their feelings of depression and guilt were worsening.

He helped them to conduct a self-evaluation about endless speculations and self-blame. They agreed that it was accomplishing nothing. They agreed to put the pain 'on hold' for one hour a day: they would do something together which incorporated effort, light conversation and at least an effort to laugh for a few minutes.

8 *No Discussion of Past Misery*
Every human body has its tender spots. When individual parts are hurting the effectiveness of the person is lessened. So too every interpersonal relationship is a system. When communication focuses on what went wrong, how things reached their current but less than pleasant state, further talk about past failures and long-standing misery adds to the pain and suffering. Intimacy is not built on the shifting sands of tribulation. Developing the attitude of 'things are the way they are because they got to be that way' helps couples to find other topics for discussion.

9 *No Criticism*
When there is stress in a relationship, it is often characterized by criticism. 'You always …' 'Why didn't you …?' 'That really gripes me …' and dozens of other stingingly critical statements regarding specific situations are uttered with unwelcome, uncomfortable and even tormenting results.

When the relationship is strained, constructive criticism is an oxymoron. The urge to speak one's mind can accelerate the downward spiral of the relationship. The characteristics of time spent together are for some the most difficult to implement. For success there must be a rule rigidly adhered to that neither party will criticize the other, that they will not engage in disputes. Rather, they will discuss 'safe', non-controversial topics. Thus, when a couple takes a brisk walk together, there is no criticism, no lectures, no admonitions, no discussion of what is good for the other person.

This is not an avoidance of serious discussion of problems. Rather, it is recommended merely because continual, one-way, worn-out lectures and criticism rarely help, and often turn off the listener. Nevertheless, it is difficult for some couples to abandon such conversation, especially if they have felt alienated. Meaningful communication, compromise and problem solving will occur and lead to intimacy if there is a solid foundation of creating and committing oneself to need-satisfying time which builds a storehouse of mutually positive perceptions and memories.

The following is an example of a couple examining their own behaviour and making helpful plans. Here Th is the therapist, H is Harry and L is Lucy.

Th: Well, I've seen you both separately a few times and you've mutually decided to talk together about how to proceed from this point.

H & L: Yes, we're ready to move on now.

Th: Just to clarify something: you've talked at length about the problems and about conflicts and about past hurts, affairs and misery?

H & L: Yes, we've rehashed those things a thousand times.

Th: Is it going to help if you continue to talk about them?

H & L: No (*they go into detail about why*).

Th: Then I think we need to take a new road. OK?

H & L: Yes.

Th: I want to ask you about how you spend your time.

H & L: (*They talk at length about how they are getting along better but spend time separately working on their own projects and so on.*)

Th: Tell me about the last time you did something enjoyable – a fun activity together without anyone else being involved.

H & L: (*They agree it has been a long time.*)

Th: I want you to talk to each other now without arguing about something you could do together which would fulfil the following conditions (*explains the components of quality time*).

L: I would like to get some exercise. There is a park nearby and we used to go there and walk for about half an hour every day.

H: I would like that, too.

L: You would?

H: Yes, it would be good. I would sleep more soundly, too.

Th: Will you do it every day for a week?

H & L: Yes.

Th: What will you avoid talking about?

H & L: (*They enumerate the items that are 'out of bounds'.*)
Th: What will you discuss?
H: How our day went.
L: How I'm different than I used to be.
Th: That's a good start. Now let's make a list of what's 'in bounds' and what's 'out of bounds'.

They make the following list:

In bounds	Out of bounds
the neighbours	the affair
the day's work	problems to face in the future
television shows	what they dislike
the children	what they get angry about
politics (they agree on this topic)	past mistakes
church (they agree on this topic)	anything blameful
jokes	complaints about other people

The session ends with specific plans for time spent together. It is important to note that the transcript is abbreviated. Also couples do not necessarily need a third person to accomplish this. They can follow this format by discussing the ideas, evaluating their current behaviours and making plans which are specific, realistic and executed immediately or soon. Part of the counselling can be an explanation of this activity as homework.

In the last analysis the amount of time, the activity and the topic for discussion are determined by the couple. This self-assessment can be enhanced with the help of a counsellor or therapist. The couples themselves decide how much overlap they have in their 'quality worlds', behaviours and perceptions. They then decide how much they wish to attain. This is followed by strategies designed to reach their agreed upon goal. Figure 4 is an activity worksheet which provides a self-assessment for discussion between partners. They are asked to determine whether the activities are enjoyable to each of them and whether they fulfill the characteristics of quality time. After completing the exercise, the crucial question to be discussed together is do or can these activities bring them closer together or further apart?

From the list below, tick the activities you enjoy. Then review the list with your partner to determine which activities fulfil the concept of **Quality Time** together. Add other suitable activities in the space at the bottom of the list, if you want to.

Activity	You	Partner
Going grocery shopping	☐	☐
Cleaning the garage	☐	☐
Taking a brisk walk	☐	☐
Taking a class together	☐	☐
Doing aerobic exercise	☐	☐
Planning a menu	☐	☐
Cooking	☐	☐
Playing card games	☐	☐
Gardening	☐	☐
Renovating furniture	☐	☐
Painting the house	☐	☐
Having sex	☐	☐
Planning a party	☐	☐
....	☐	☐
....	☐	☐
....	☐	☐
....	☐	☐
....	☐	☐

Figure 4: *Quality Time Relationship Chart*

Level B: Communication, Conversation

It is impossible for couples to fail to communicate. Total silence and shunning each other's company is a strong form of communication. The message delivered in this way might even be effective in communicating displeasure, dislike, anger, resentment, rage and a host of other signals. But, while the effort might be effective, the goal of intimacy is defeated.

Helpful communication in Reality Therapy is not radically different from that commonly accepted by therapists, such as using 'I messages'. Still there are some additions based on the formulation summarized by the letters WDEP.

W. Couples describe what they want. They talk about what they want in such areas as profession/career, family, personal, financial, intellectual, recreational and spiritual.

D. Couples discuss many aspects of their current behaviour, that is, what they are doing. The action component of the behavioural system is only one aspect of conversation, however. Others include what each person thinks, how they feel and even their physiology. The last component seems to assume more prominence as the years take their toll. But it is the action component which it is useful to emphasize in enhancing relational closeness. In building relationships emphasis is put on discussing common interests, areas of agreement and activities which are pleasant. This in no way implies that evasive behaviour, or the defence mechanisms of minimizing, denying or shunning controversy are encouraged. It means that intimacy begins and is founded on common ground, similar quality worlds and a common behavioural direction.

Feelings are, of course, the topic of conversation in many communication workshops. Couples are encouraged to be frank and open, to share their feelings. 'Don't suppress or deny how you feel' is the admonition. In Reality Therapy, however, couples are encouraged to talk about feelings only in connection with actions. These are not separated as definitively as in some methods. The reason is that feelings are seen as behaviours. The causes of behaviour are rooted in the quality world, that is, the wants of the person. Also the feelings can be used to bring people together when the communication is related to what each person does with the anger, impatience, irritation, depression and so on. Further, plans for current or future resolution of upsetting feelings can be made when discussing actions. Conversely, joy, excitement, friendliness, tolerance and empathy can be prolonged and used to facilitate the intimacy if they are linked to what each person is doing within the relationship. Two people become a system when they interact with each other. Also, when they translate the feelings into wants, efforts can be made to resolve differences, lessen the intensity of negative feelings and increase the positive ones.

Below is a dialogue between a two-career couple which illustrates the above principles. Sam is a 35-year-old junior executive for a computer information company. Meg is a sales representative for a dental equipment company. Meg comes home after a very difficult day attempting to sell equipment and supplies to dentists in her area. Sam is already at home and is watching TV. Here S is Sam and M is Meg. Meg enters the house, walks in with a heavy tread and drops her purse and briefcase on the floor in the living room.

S: Not a good day, huh?

M: I don't want to talk about it.

S: That bad?

M: Worse. I'm fed up with Shelby (*Shelby is the manager*). And some **!#@* almost hit me on the motorway.

S: Do you need some time to settle down? (*Turns off his favourite TV programme.*)

M: I'll tell you later. You don't need to turn off the TV.

S: It's OK. I don't need to watch it. Besides, I'd rather be with you for a few minutes.

M: Sometimes you don't even want me to talk when that soap's on. You don't even know I'm in the room sometimes. That's another thing.

S: I think I've been a little remote lately and put you on 'hold' when *Coronation Street*'s on.

M: Don't give me that 'I'm guilty' crap.

S: OK, but I really do want to hear what happened today.

M: I've been selling like crazy lately, as I've told you. But I don't want to dump the other stuff on you.

S: Maybe you need a little time to calm down. I can see you're upset. You have that steely look on your face that tells me you are really upset.

M: (*Smiles slightly.*) Give me a half-hour to change clothes, wash and get my briefcase in order. Why don't you watch your show?

S: I don't need to. Do you need any help?

M: You could rub my back.

S: It'll be a pleasure.

In the above segment Sam reads Meg's non-verbal behaviour and reflects on it. He is aware that for her doing something alone might help even more than ventilating her feelings. He does not attempt to impose this on her but he asks her about her own quality world at the moment: does she think she needs some time to settle down, time to be alone but not completely alone? He is there in close proximity and is available. He even gives up a high-priority want, watching his favourite TV programme, as a selfless gesture in order to be available to Meg if she decides to talk. Clearly upset about what happened today, she links her unpleasant anger-inducing experience with her previously unexpressed annoyance, even anger, at him for putting his TV programme before her.

Sam accepts the criticism, refuses to be defensive and declines to attack back. From much experience he knows that it is easy to make the situation worse by trying to win. Still angry, Meg jabs him again with the remark about his guilty feelings. Sam does not add fuel to the fire by justifying his statement which, in fact, might have been based on guilt. Rather he says, 'OK, but I really do want to hear what happened today.' Instead of elaborating on his own behaviour, he shares his quality world using 'I messages' rather than attacking. These behaviours can be taught directly by a Reality Therapist and are more likely to be implemented if built on quality time.

Note: This is a major principle in using the WDEP system of Reality Therapy effectively: instead of justifying one's own action, it is often useful to share one's quality world, especially if the picture in the quality world (want) at that moment includes the best interest of the other person.

From past experience, Sam knows that the quality world of Meg, when she is upset, includes support but not encouragement, and physical nearness, but not hovering over her. Because he is willing to 'be there' for her she asks for physical contact to help her relax. She also appreciates his willingness to be there for her 100 per cent and not turn on the television. She recognizes that he is able to read her deeper quality world picture (want) for him to attend to her rather than the want for him to meet his own needs by watching the TV.

The dialogue continues:

S: What do you want me to do now? I would like to do something that would really help.

M: Just rub my back and listen.

S: That's fine, what do you want to get off your mind first?

Meg goes into detail about her hurt and anger at the manager who wants her to break in a new sales rep who is too flirtatious with her and who will be awarded some of the territory which she has developed. To make matters worse, the manager is a decent and fair-minded person who is honest and has the welfare of the company at heart. Meg also states that the issue would be less troublesome if he were a jerk. To top it all off, she almost had a crash on the motorway which would have been her fault. 'But the bloke should have seen me,' she adds.

At this point Sam could take either of two directions in his communication. He could help her develop a plan to talk to the supervisor about the territory. She could also discuss the behaviour of the new sales rep, which is not too threatening but which is rather annoying. He could help her deal directly with the sales rep in order to solve this vexing problem. But Sam is aware of her quality world, having made many mistakes by trying to impose his 'get to a solution' mentality on her. Instead he listens carefully and empathically not only to her feelings, but to her self-talk and what she has done regarding these aggravations. He hears her annoyance and connects it with the fact that she is expecting too much from the company as well as expecting reasonable behaviour from the sales rep. He reflects on what she has done by reminding her gently that she is a high flyer for the company and they are really quite proud to have her in their employ. He knows that at all costs he needs to avoid the 'How are you going to work it out?', 'What's your plan?', 'We need to develop a strategy' approach. That is for later!

Meg at this moment seems to be making choices related to belonging. If Sam can connect on that level they will get closer as a couple. But if Sam were to take the problem-solving approach he would be misreading her need, at the moment, as need for power and for control or for freedom from the stress and strain of the situation. Her real need is belonging. The signs and cues are not easy to read and Sam might take a long time learning them. But if he uses his ears and mouth in a two-to-one proportion he has made a major step.

The above example of Sam and Meg illustrates how a couple can interact at a high level. This interdependence is based on a solid foundation – the habitual commitment to spend time together which is characterized by the building blocks in Figure 3, page 82.

Level A: Problem Solving, Resolving Power Struggles, Compromise and Decision Making

Use of E and P
At Level A the couple strategizes about problems, power issues, compromises and decisions. Emphasized are both E (evaluation of wants, actions, perceptions and future behaviours) and P (plans which are realistically doable and mutually satisfying).

It is clear that there is no absolute distinction between levels B and A. At level A, however, the focus with Sam and Meg is on the following questions:

- 'How can we plan to improve the situation at work?'

- 'How can we solve our differences without rancour and so that each of us fulfils at least part of our quality worlds?'

- 'What specifically can we do to address the problems which we face?'

- 'What will each of us need to give up in order to make the best decisions?'

- 'How will our decisions be satisfying to each of us?'

The above open-ended and thought-provoking questions are most effectively addressed when there is a solid foundation of levels B, C and D.

Using what you have learned from this book so far about Choice Therapy and Reality Therapy, you are invited to write a successful future scenario for Sam and Meg.

CHAPTER 9

Reality Therapy and Addictions Treatment

R EALITY THERAPY IS a method that has been used extensively in addictions treatment since the early 1970s and again, particularly in North America, it has been widely used in conjunction with the 'Minnesota Method' of treatment and other treatment programmes that also utilize the Twelve Steps of the Anonymous Fellowships. This does not mean that Reality Therapy as a method is linked to the 'Twelve Steps' in any 'formal' way, only that it is a method that can be (and has been) successfully implemented with such programmes.

Applicability to Addictions Treatment
The reasons for Reality Therapy's high applicability to addictions counselling and treatment include the following:

1   The necessity for a very focused counselling approach, particularly in the earliest stages of recovery, whereby possibly life-threatening substance abuse behaviours can be confronted and issues of denial can be addressed. Without the need for a hostile or aggressive approach by the counsellor, Reality Therapy's questioning style and its adherence to personal responsibility can provide a very necessary focus on the client's *current* (total) behaviours and, in the first instance, help them to curtail their drinking, or use of drugs, or other addictive behaviours, such as gambling, eating disorders, workaholism, sex and love addiction or compulsive helping.

2   The *delivery system* of Reality Therapy (the WDEP system) is one that is readily applicable to the processes and approaches used in the vast majority of treatment programmes. This is the case whether such counselling is conducted in groups or in one-to-one counselling, or indeed some combination of the two.

3   Reality Therapy, as a counselling approach, remains highly applicable through all the stages of recovery (as described by Gorski, 1985), from the 'transition' (or 'pre-treatment') stage, where the person begins to recognize they have problems with chemicals or other addictive behaviours, through to both 'maintenance' (of sobriety/abstinence) and relapse prevention, where the ability of people to meet their basic needs effectively and continuously will correlate strongly with their continued success in sobriety/abstinence.

4   In more recent years, research studies have reported the effectiveness of cognitive behavioural approaches of counselling and addictions treatment, in both group and individual therapy.

By far the largest, most significant and, without doubt, the most expensive research study to date (with a reported cost of some $27 million) has been that conducted by the USA's National Institute on Alcohol Abuse and Alcoholism. The NIAAA's study is referred to as 'Project Match' ('Matching Alcoholism Treatments to Client Heterogenicity: Project MATCH; Post-treatment Drinking Outcomes, 1997'). Their earliest research findings, published in 1997, reported the effectiveness of cognitive behavioural coping skills as well as that of 'Twelve Step Facilitation' and 'Motivational Enhancement Therapy' – the two other modalities used in the project.

Obviously the results of how the participating 1,726 patients progress will be monitored over the years to come. However, it is our assessment that the continuity of treatment and undoubted sense of *belonging, connectedness* and *support* provided by 'Twelve-Step Facilitation', plus its emphasis on treating the 'spiritual disease' within (a more holistic approach overall), will prove to be the most successful of the three modalities *in the longer term*. This last comment is not intended to belittle cognitive behavioural therapy (Reality Therapy is a cognitive behavioural therapy) nor Motivational Enhancement Therapy. Rather it is intended to stress our experience and belief that Reality Therapy (as well as other cognitive behavioural approaches) will usually (but not always) be most effective in addictions treatment when it is combined with a long-term programme that provides on-going support and a real sense of *belonging* and *acceptance*. Without doubt this is something which Twelve-Step programmes provide (eg, the Anonymous Fellowships) and, of course, they are most certainly long-term! This point regarding the effectiveness of integrating Reality Therapy into a long-term and comprehensive treatment programme(s), as in the Minnesota Method, is something which will be further emphasized in this chapter.

Lastly, with regards to research studies in the field of addictions, Reality Therapy has been reported to be an effective and successful counselling approach in several studies; notably those by Chance (1990) and by Honeyman (1990). However, the need for longer-term and more in-depth research is most certainly apparent.

Getting it into Perspective
The overview that will be provided in this chapter of a Choice Theory understanding of addiction and the Reality Therapy approach to counselling in addictions treatment is written primarily for the benefit of those already working in the addictions field (to enhance their skill and effectiveness) and for those contemplating doing so in the future, as well as, of course, for general interest.

However, it is by no means intended to provide an in-depth understanding of addiction and its treatment, nor a 'stand alone' guide to addictions counselling. Indeed, we would vigorously emphasize the importance of acquiring a thorough understanding of substance abuse, of addictive behaviour patterns, of the stages of recovery and their implications, and of the issues applicable to relapse prevention, before becoming engaged in counselling an addicted person.

Indeed, the view is held strongly by many people working in addictions treatment (and who are in recovery themselves) that it is possible to learn *about* addiction and its treatment, but impossible to really *understand* addiction unless one has been through treatment and is in recovery oneself. Be that as it may, it is our own experience and belief that effective addictions counselling is not dependent simply on one being in recovery oneself, even if it can be an advantage. Further, we hope that the overview that follows will be of practical value to anyone currently working in this field or who plans to do so in the future, and that they may be interested enough to pursue Reality Therapy training specific to addictions treatment at some future time.

Addiction: A Genetic Predisposition or Learned Behaviour?

In addition to the above, it is important to emphasize that it is not the intention of this chapter to get involved in the *genetic disease versus learned behaviour* debate that has engulfed treatment provision for many years. There are those who fervently support the notion that addiction is a *genetic predisposition* (in other words, an inherited disease state), while others, who oppose this notion, claim that addiction is an 'acquired' or 'learned' behaviour, specific to the substance or behaviour in question; that it has biopsychosocial determinants and that it can cause the onset of disease states (such as cirrhosis of the liver, cancer or heart disease).

With regard to the practice of Reality Therapy in addictions treatment, it makes no difference whether one believes that addiction is genetically inherited or not. The Reality Therapist is always working with *current reality* and when an addicted person comes for counselling or treatment, their current reality is that they have a (perhaps, potentially life-threatening) addiction and they need help – now!

How the person 'got there' (genetic predisposition or not) makes little or no difference with regard to the treatment they need now, which very broadly speaking is to stop or curtail the addictive behaviour; to go through the process of detoxification, as and when necessary; and, thereafter, gradually to begin rebuilding their lives, while maintaining total abstinence – invariably lifelong. Reality Therapy can play an effective role throughout the whole of this treatment process, but most prominently in respect of the person coming to terms with their current reality (their addiction) and in helping them to begin rebuilding their life for a better today and tomorrow.

From a Choice Theory perspective, rebuilding one's life means beginning to fulfil one's *basic needs* in a healthy and satisfying way and, in particular, to 'connect' or 'reconnect' with people who can provide love and care, trust, acceptance and support. For many people in recovery, of course, at least part of that 'connection' is found in their association and regular attendance at the Anonymous Fellowship meetings.

A Choice Theory Understanding of Addictive Behaviour

Whether one believes that addiction is a genetically inherited disease or learned behaviour, the Choice Theory explanation for a person 'choosing' or generating behaviours to the extent that they become addictive is compatible.

People choose such behaviours (drinking, drugs, food, sex, gambling and so on) in an attempt to fulfil a profound sense of *inner emptiness*. And that inner emptiness is created by their continual inability to satisfy or fulfil one or more of their basic needs (love and belonging, power/self-worth, freedom, fun and survival) or when one or more of their needs has been violated in some way, as in the emotional trauma of loss or bereavement, abandonment or abuse.

One of these unfulfilled or violated needs will always be love and belonging (that is, they have become 'disconnected' from a person or group of people whom they very much care about or want to be 'connected' to and/or they have no satisfying relationships in their life now). Another need that frequently accompanies the unfulfilment of love and belonging is power/self-worth. Moreover, once addiction takes a hold, addicted people always come to feel 'powerless' over their lives.

Examples include the following:

- the person who starts drinking after their partner leaves them (love and belonging) or after they lose their job (power/self-worth; plus, perhaps belonging, freedom, fun and the threat to 'survival');
- the lonely, 'disconnected' (love and belonging) and bored (fun need) person who attempts to fill their emptiness with recreational drugs;
- the person who yearns for love and attention (love and belonging) and respect and positive regard (power/self-worth) from their

parents or family or significant others, but finds they cannot get it unconditionally and so generates an eating disorder (or some other behaviour) in an attempt to get what they need, and thereby fill the emptiness;

- the people who generate or choose all the other behaviours (gambling, sex, compulsive helping, shopping, workaholism and so on) in an attempt to fill this inner void.

So, to be clear with regard to a Choice Theory explanation in respect of the 'disease concept'; if there is such a thing as a genetic predisposition to addiction, such disposition alone does not cause the addiction. Rather, it is *triggered* by the inner emptiness created by continuous unfulfilled needs, and predominantly the needs for love and belonging and power/self-worth. The behaviours that are then chosen (drinking, drugs, food, gambling and so on) are then more likely to become addictive if the person has such a genetic predisposition.

Added to this, we know that any substance or behaviour that has the capacity to change one's mood state is potentially addictive to somebody; and invariably the greater the mood-changing capacity or strength, the greater the potential for addiction.

Mood Changes and Illusions

Ultimately, all human beings are motivated to move towards pleasure and away from pain. Likewise, what we know for sure is that the purpose of all addictive behaviours is 'to feel better': to lift the depressing mood, to feel more 'in control', to feel more sociable and outgoing, to feel more 'connected' to other people, to drown the sorrows, to fill the emptiness.

And of course, initially at least, it works. But not long enough. Soon the emptiness returns and we are right back where we started. So the addictive cycle begins again; only, in time, the 'cycle' becomes a 'spiral' and down and down we go. Feeling good and being 'in control' becomes an illusion. Indeed, with regard to a Choice Theory understanding of addictive behaviour, the illusions created in addiction permeate all aspects of the Choice Theory model. To clarify this, let us look at a case study related to alcohol abuse.

Case Study: Jim

Jim, always known to be a 'heavy drinker', radically increased his alcohol consumption over a year ago when his wife finally left him (a violation of his need for love and belonging). Owing to his high absenteeism and deteriorating performance at work, he also lost his job a few months thereafter (violating his needs for power/self-worth and survival).

The devastating sense of inner emptiness is now only drowned when Jim is under the influence of alcohol. During these times Jim has the illusion that all of his needs are being adequately satisfied: his need for *love and belonging* is met either by his drinking pals or by his reliable, non-judgemental, trustworthy and comforting 'forever friend', alias his next drink. Moreover, when he is drinking it feels like the whole world loves him. He begins to perceive that he is 'in control' of his life (*power/self-worth*) and completely free (*freedom need*) of any problems or cares. While he is drinking *fun and enjoyment* abound and even his *health and survival* problems seem to disappear.

The dominant 'pictures' in Jim's 'quality world' become the drink itself, the pubs and clubs he frequents and the people he drinks with. Other (previously important) 'quality world pictures' have faded into insignificance. Jim's perception is, of course, equally affected and he soon comes to put a negative or neutral perceptual value on most things in his life except the next drink. Indeed, with the urge to drink so frequently overwhelming his entire being, Jim's 'total behaviour' (his one-track thinking, his erratic actions, his roller-coaster feelings and his craving physiology) is soon sadly and devastatingly under the influence of his illusory friend.

The Reality Therapy Approach in Addictions Treatment

In brief, the goal of the Reality Therapist is to help Jim to stop drinking, to undergo detoxification, if necessary, to commit himself to a programme of recovery, and gradually to begin rebuilding his life by replacing alcohol with more healthy (needs-satisfying) wants in his 'quality world'. Essential in such positive change would be helping Jim to 'connect' or 'reconnect' with people who would care about and support him (including, perhaps, the 'connectedness' that can be experienced by regular attendance at AA); and helping Jim to begin putting a negative perceptual value on any future use of alcohol and to follow through on plans (initially 'just for today') that would be as 'needs-satisfying' as possible, while maintaining total abstinence from alcohol.

Having given the above brief overview of a Reality Therapy approach in the treatment of alcoholism, an essential question to raise is whether clients need the same degree of help no matter where they are in recovery. The amount of intervention depends not only on the knowledge and skill of the therapist but also on the client's stage of development in recovery, and it is to this that we now turn.

Reality Therapy Applied to the Stages of Recovery

Although a variety of very useful models of recovery exist, one which we have found to be particularly comprehensive is Terence Gorski's six stage 'Developmental Model of Recovery' (Gorski, 1985). Again, although this is an overview, we hope it gives the reader a good understanding of how the six stages apply to the WDEP system of Reality Therapy. Keep in mind that the stages are not totally separate; rather, one merges into another.

The Transition Stage

Here clients learn that their lives have become unmanageable, but invariably they believe that they are not addicted. They say to themselves: 'I use alcohol or drugs [or other behaviours] because I have life problems. If the problems would go away, I would be able to stop using.'

If they can begin a treatment programme or find help in sorting out what is really going on, most addicted people come to recognize that it is their substance or behavioural misuse that is now causing the greatest problems. However, many will hold on to the belief that, when they finally straighten out their lives, they will be able to drink or use again. This secret belief often leads them to relapse later in recovery.

During this stage the Reality Therapist stresses the client's actions and acts as a psychological mirror confronting the client in a firm (but not hostile or aggressive) manner and allowing the client or family to describe substance-related behaviours and their effect on people significant to the client. The counsellor creates a firm yet friendly atmosphere, balancing confrontation with support.

Because 'recognition' (that the person has an addiction) is a key issue in this transition stage, the use of self-assessment questionnaires can be extremely useful, and several very good sources are available for referral and use: notably, Lefever (1988) and Gorski (1989). Indeed, more recently, Dr Robert Lefever has written a very thought-provoking and comprehensive book, *Inside the Madness* (Lefever, 1997) that would be of great benefit to both counsellors and patients with regard to their recognition and understanding of addictive behaviour.

Stabilization Stage

Clients need now to deal with withdrawal and later to develop a recognition (or identity) of their being an alcoholic, or chemically and/or behaviourally addicted. Gorski (1985) says that for some clients this stage can last up to two years.

Clients need support and encouragement as they overcome withdrawal and start learning to solve problems without the use of alcohol or other drugs. As in the transition stage, the client's denial is still very apparent (usually to everyone except themselves) and the counsellor again addresses this by reflecting back the client's past and present behaviours (the 'D' of the WDEP system) and providing observations and feedback, pointing out what seems to have worked and not worked. It should be emphasized again that at this stage clients are not always capable of making their own self-evaluations and so need help. Obviously, when facilitating a group, such observations, evaluations and feedback are invariably provided by the other members of the group, usually with significant impact!

Early Recovery Stage

This is a time of internal change, when clients learn on a deeper level that they cannot use alcohol or drugs. They begin to heal the inner psychological damage created by the addiction; they work to overcome feelings of shame, guilt and remorse; and they learn to handle stress more effectively.

The Reality Therapist recognizes that clients can self-evaluate more effectively and continues to help them to live one day at a time by encouraging more independent self-evaluations.

Middle Recovery Stage

During this stage, life (as well as counselling) becomes centred on issues other than alcohol or drugs. The Reality Therapist helps clients to deal with doubt about whether sobriety is worthwhile. Clients begin to undergo life-style changes and learn how to repair past damage and try to put balance back into their lives. They face marriage/relationship and family problems and decisions which have been submerged until now.

Reality Therapy is now applied to issues relating more comprehensively to the satisfaction of basic needs and most importantly, as previously stated, 'connecting' and 'reconnecting' with people significant to the client.

The teaching of Choice Theory (which virtually any person can readily understand and relate to) is recognized by the Reality Therapist as being of immense practical (lifelong) value for all clients, and would certainly be introduced at this stage.

Late Recovery and Maintenance Stages

Clients move even further beyond the issues of sobriety and dependency. They focus on overcoming obstacles to healthy living that they may have learned as children (particularly so if they came from dysfunctional families) and deal with further family issues, learning to share their inner resources with family and community. They move beyond a narrow and all-pervading one-day-at-a-time attitude. They still commit themselves to one-day-at-a-time, but they learn to make longer-range plans without a preoccupation with alcohol, drugs or other addictive behaviours. We agree with Gorski (1985) that not everyone needs counselling at the late recovery and/or maintenance stages, but acknowledge that everyone needs support and 'connectedness' with other people throughout this time and beyond.

In summary, the lines of distinction between the various stages of recovery are not precise and, likewise, a client's progress through the stages cannot be calculated or predicted with any degree of precision. Reality Therapy as a method of counselling is certainly applicable to all of the stages, but – as explained above – needs to be applied differently in the earlier stages than it does in the later stages.

An overriding principle in using Reality Therapy in the early stages of recovery, when the client deals with sobriety issues and day-to-day living, is that the counsellor should be very specific in helping clients to evaluate their behavioural direction and in making plans. The counsellor does this in three ways:

1   providing observations and feedback, pointing out what seems to have worked and not worked;
2   asking more 'closed' evaluation questions: for example, 'Does socializing with your old drinking pals and hanging out at your old drinking haunts increase or decrease the likelihood that you'll drink again?';
3   offering suggestions for specific and shorter-range plans more often than in the later stages of recovery.

In the later stages, the Reality Therapist asks more 'open' self-evaluation questions and helps the client to begin rebuilding their life in a more needs-satisfying way, without the preoccupation with alcohol, drugs or other addictive behaviours. Clients now have some history of sobriety and a database for knowing what is helpful and what is harmful. They have experience of more effective planning. In short, they have come to develop a perceived internal locus of control and internal standards which serve as a basis for self-initiated evaluations and plan making, into the stage of maintenance and, therefore, it is hoped, for the rest of their lives.

CHAPTER 10

Paradoxical Techniques

IT HAS BEEN SAID THAT there are no resistant clients, only unimaginative therapists. Perhaps current theory and practice in the helping professions have not developed ways to deal with resistance which are 100 per cent effective. On the other hand, human beings choose their behaviour and they cannot be manoeuvred into better choices, no matter how inventive the counsellor might be if they are determined not to change. Still, there are creative interventions for dealing with resistance which are congruent with Reality Therapy. These are called paradoxical techniques.

Definition and Origin
A paradox is an apparent contradiction, something which seems to be false but which is true. The Bible is filled with many paradoxes, such as 'It is in giving that we receive', 'The first shall be last, the last shall be first' and 'In order to gain life we must lose it.' And so on.

In therapy, paradoxical techniques have been used with such problems as anorexia, dizziness, encopresis, hysterical blindness, chronic pain, phobias, sexual problems and sleep disorders.

In other theories paradox is given various names, such as antisuggestion, joining the resistance, supporting the defences, outcrazying the patient, implosion, flooding, paradoxical intention, restraining and predicting (Steltzer, 1986). Milton Erickson and Viktor Frankl are two names traditionally associated with paradoxical techniques.

Types of Paradox

There are two kinds of paradox which are especially useful in Reality Therapy: reframing and prescription.

Reframing

It is often useful for counsellors to see the point of view of the client, but it can be equally helpful to think differently from the client. Getting locked into the client's perception might actually facilitate the continuance of the problem, whereas giving the behaviour or problem a new meaning can be useful. For the sake of practice, a list of behaviours is provided below. In the column on the right, reframe the behaviour from negative to positive (or less negative). Do not be concerned about exact meanings. The meaning changes when it is relabelled.

1	Aggressive	becomes	*for example: energetic*
2	Passive	becomes	*for example: relaxed*
3	Stingy	becomes	*for example: thrifty*
4	Arrogant	becomes	
5	Shy	becomes	
6	Hyperactive	becomes	
7	Melancholic	becomes	
8	Dysfunctional	becomes	
9	Incoherent	becomes	
10	Narcissistic	becomes	

The above activity is intended to provide practice in thinking paradoxically. It does not suggest that all of these behaviours should at all times be seen in a positive light.

Central to reframing is to give the behaviour new meaning or to remove the meaning from it. Reframing can take many forms such as in the following example.

In a middle school there existed a problem in the girls' cloakroom. There was a group of girls who regularly wrote on the mirror and would kiss it, leaving lipstick marks all over it. The staff repeatedly tried to catch the girls, but they eluded detection. Then one day the maintenance person, who was a woman, entered the washroom and found the mirror in its usual condition. Five or six girls were standing around talking. They happened to be the group who were the suspected girls. The woman merely took her long brush, went over to the toilet, and dipped it in the bowl. She proceeded to clean the lipstick off the mirror while telling the girls, 'This is how I clean the mirrors.' After that there were no lip marks on the mirror for the remainder of the school year. Other examples of reframing are congratulating the family who come for counselling: they have taken a step upwards; saying to the woman who was sacked from 10 jobs in a year, 'You have an excellent skill at finding jobs'; describing even a five per cent improvement as a big step forward.

The ability to reframe is part of the repertoire of the Reality Therapist. The effective user of the WDEP system has the talent for seeing the negative as positive, for seeing issues and problems as advantages. This ability or talent is not inborn. It is developed by consultation and practice.

Prescription

The second paradoxical technique, prescription, is more subtle and requires both skill and creativity, *as well as much caution*. It is not used casually or impetuously. The prescription, sometimes known as a directive or an ordeal, is used when linear planning is ineffective (Weeks & L'Abate, 1982). The counsellor suggests that the problem behaviour be chosen. For example, in the classic video training tape, 'Woman with Psychosomatic Problems' (1975), Glasser attempts to help a woman talk about issues other than her problems. She insists on talking about her aches and pains. Glasser encourages her to list them one by one, even though of itself this recitation would be seen by many as non-therapeutic. But she believes she will solve the problems by talking about them. He then remarks that she could talk about them to him but she was not to complain at work or to her boyfriend. In other words, the symptom is not prescribed indiscriminately.

Very often the plan is prescribed with a concomitant aversive behaviour attached. One client, rejected by his girlfriend, felt compelled to call her every day. However, he wanted to stop this painful and self-defeating behaviour. The counsellor did not encourage him to call her but suggested that, every time he did call her, he should write a cheque to a cause he did not agree with. After several cheques paid to a distasteful organization, he ceased the phone calls.

Below is a list of behaviours. You are asked to assume that linear plans have not worked. List prescriptive plans for each behaviour. The plans should be done only for short periods.

Person worrying about moving from one part of the country to another:

Example plan: to put 'on hold' the urge to worry during the day, but then between 6.30 to 7.00 pm to have a concentrated worry session about everything that could possibly go wrong.

Person who feels compelled to return to the house at least three times to check the cooker:

Example plan: that each time they leave the house they must come back in again, check the cooker and then go out again, locking the door behind them. However, they must repeat this activity eight times.

Person who panics before giving speeches:

_____

_____

_____

_____

_____

_____

Person with hand-washing compulsion:

_____

_____

_____

_____

_____

_____

Person who is a habitual complainer:

_____

_____

_____

_____

_____

_____

Person who blushes:

_____

_____

_____

_____

_____

Person who cannot sleep at night:

_____

_____

_____

_____

_____

Child who has temper tantrums:

_____

_____

_____

_____

_____

The above examples are listed for practice. There is no implication that prescriptions should be used each time these behaviours are presented in counselling. Linear plans are used before paradoxical plans are attempted.

Even in these practice sessions and in all prescriptive plans, the directive is often scheduled at a precise time and for a limited period; sometimes even for just a few seconds. For instance, if the client blushes, suggest trying to make it worse for 15 to 20 seconds. This is the opposite of trying to fight it which invariably worsens the problem. Also, this is used in connection with the self-evaluation component (of the WDEP system). If fighting the blush does not help, another course of action could be more effective.

The habitual complainer who wants to complain less could choose to set aside 10 minutes for concentrated complaining, preferably while alone. There would be no-one to provide sympathy, empathy or support. The perception of impacting or manoeuvring others would be absent. The pay off vanishes, the person very often feels a greater sense of conscious control over their previously habitual behaviour (often choosing to relinquish or lessen the behaviour) and, most importantly, as in all uses of paradoxical actions, no harm is done to self or others.

Ethical Guidelines

Before using paradoxical techniques, especially the prescription, a thorough knowledge of ethical principles is advised.

1   Follow-through would not be harmful. Any suggested prescription should not result in harm if the client implements the plan. The plan is not suggested if the performance of it will result in danger or harm. Thus suicidal persons are not encouraged to spend 10 minutes thinking about suicide; drug takers are not admonished to take drugs; obesity is not addressed by eating more; vomiting is not suggested to the bulimic client; the arsonist is not encouraged to set fires.

    The counsellor could ask themselves the question suggested by Corey (1998): would you want your suggestion to be made public? If publicizing it would be an embarrassment, it might be better to take a different approach with the client.

2   There should be a trusting relationship present before prescriptions are given. If there is little trust, the client tends to view the paradox

as manipulation. In fact, a major criticism of paradoxical techniques is that they are manipulative. If they are used by an irresponsible therapist, this criticism is justified.

3   Paradox should be avoided when clients are of a suspicious nature. Even mild cases of paranoia can be exacerbated when such clients are told to make things worse.

4   Acute crises are not occasions for implementing paradoxical techniques. In times of grief, family tragedies, loss of employment or financial disasters, appropriate interventions include empathy, support and linear planning.

5   Paradoxical techniques are used extensively in family therapy, But anyone using such techniques should be trained in systems theory and use prescriptions only with supervision or consultation. Weeks and L'Abate (1982) warn against using it in families where there is inconsistency and turmoil. Family use of paradox is most effective when there are already existing patterns of behaviour. Families which project most of the responsibility onto others are not good candidates for paradoxical interventions, nor are families where hostility is a theme.

In summary, paradoxical interventions are useful in the practice of Reality Therapy, but they should be used with caution, circumspection and at times with supervision.

Basis for Paradoxical Interventions

While the use of paradoxical techniques is characteristic of many theories, Choice Theory and Reality Therapy offer a clear explanation of these techniques' effectiveness. In Choice Theory the purpose of all behaviour is to control, to affect, and to manoeuvre the external world in the hope that it will match internal desires or quality world pictures (Glasser, 1980, 1984, 1998). Thus, if a mother advises her daughter or son to have a temper tantrum, the child's choice to control the parent becomes less effective. The child no longer controls the adult.

In an opposite sense, when clients feel victimized by worries, fears, panic or phobias, they gain the perception of control by explicitly choosing the behaviour. They no longer feel dominated by the problem: on the contrary, they now have control of the symptom and, if they can choose it, they can choose to relinquish it. This is the ultimate paradox.

The exciting and often effective techniques summarized in this chapter should be used as condiments: they are not the main course of a meal. Still, they can make the meal tasty and a successful dining experience.

References

Baird J, 'Conservation of the commons: effects of group cohesiveness and prior sharing', *Journal of Community Psychology* 10, pp210–215, 1982.

Brickell J, 'The reality of stress and pressure', *Counselling News,* 18–19 September 1992.

Brickell J & Wubbolding R, 'Reality Therapy and Addiction', *One to One* 7, p15, National Association of Alcohol and Drug Abuse Counsellors (United Kingdom), 1995.

Brickell J & Wubbolding R, 'How You Can Use Reality Therapy in Addictions Treatment', *Addictions Counselling World,* Sept/Oct, pp19–22, 1996.

Chance E, 'Lifeline: a drug/alcohol treatment program for negatively addicted inmates', *Journal of Reality Therapy* 9(2), pp33–38, 1990.

Cockrum R, 'Reality Therapy: Interviews with Dr William Glasser', *Psychology* 26(1), pp13–16, 1989.

Cockrum R, *The Relationship Questionnaire,* Quality Development Seminars, Louisville, 1994.

Corey G, *Theory and Practice of Group Counseling,* Brooks Cole Publishers, Pacific Grove, CA, 1995.

Corey G, Corey MA & Callanan P, *Issues and Ethics in the Helping Professions,* Brooks Cole Publishers, Pacific Grove, CA, 1998.

Deming W, *Out of the Crisis,* Massachusetts Institute of Technology, Center for Advanced Engineering Study, Cambridge, MA, 1984.

Dreikurs R, *Maintaining Sanity in the Classroom,* Harper & Row, New York, 1972.

Edelwich J, *Burn-out,* Human Sciences Press, New York, 1980.

Ethical Standards for Group Counsellors, Association for Specialists in Group Work, American Association for Counseling and Development, Alexandria, VA, 1989.

Fahrney M & Pettie P, 'The interrelationship of the principles of Reality Therapy and group dynamics', *Journal of Reality Therapy* 6(2), pp10–18, 1987.

Ford E, *For the Love of Children*, Doubleday, New York, 1977.

Ford E, *Permanent Love*, Winston, Minneapolis, 1979.

Ford E, *Choosing to Love*, HarperCollins, New York, 1983.

Glasser C, *My Quality World Workbook*, The William Glasser Institute, Chatsworth, CA, 1996a.

Glasser C, *My Quality World Activity Set*, The William Glasser Institute, Chatsworth, CA, 1996b.

Glasser W, *Reality Therapy, A New Approach to Psychiatry*, HarperCollins, New York, 1965.

Glasser W, *Schools Without Failure*, HarperCollins, New York, 1968.

Glasser W, 'Woman with Psychosomatic Problems', video. The William Glasser Institute, Chatsworth, CA, 1975.

Glasser W, *Stations of the Mind*, HarperCollins, New York, 1981.

Glasser W, *Control Theory*, HarperCollins, New York, 1984.

Glasser W, *A Diagram of the Brain as a Control System*, The William Glasser Institute, Los Angeles, 1986.

Glasser W, *The Quality School*, HarperCollins, New York, 1990.

Glasser W, *The Quality School Teacher*, HarperCollins, New York, 1993.

Glasser W, *Control Theory Manager*, HarperCollins, New York, 1994.

Glasser W, *Staying Together*, HarperCollins, New York, 1995.

Glasser W, *Choice Theory*, HarperCollins, New York, 1996.

Glasser W, *Choice Theory, A New Psychology of Personal Freedom*, HarperCollins, New York, 1998.

Glasser W, Programs, Policies and Procedures of The William Glasser Institute, The William Glasser Institute, Chatsworth, CA, 1999.

Glasser W & Wubbolding R, 'Reality Therapy', Corsini R (ed), *Current Psychotherapies,* Peacock Press, Itasca, IL, 1995.

Gorski T, *The Developmental Model of Recovery*, Access Publications, Indianapolis, IN, 1985.

Gorski T, *Passages Through Recovery*, Hazeldon Recovery Series, HarperCollins, New York, 1989.

Greene B, *New Paradigms*, New View, Chapel Hill, 1995.

Herlihy B & Golden L, *Ethical Standards Casebook,* American Counseling Association, Alexandria, VA, 1996.

Hoglund R, *The School for Quality Learning,* Research Press, Champaign, IL, 1993.

Honeyman A, 'Perceptual changes in addicts as a consequence of Reality Therapy based on group treatment', *Journal of Reality Therapy* 9(2), pp53–9, 1990.

Jennings J, 'Multiple approaches to the treatment of violent couples', *American Journal of Family Therapy* 19(4), pp351–361, 1991.

Kaiser H, 'The problem of responsibility in psychotherapy', *Psychiatry* 18, pp205–11 in *Effective Psychotherapy.* Frierman L, (ed), Macmillan, New York, 1965.

Kohn A, *Punished by Rewards,* Houghton Mifflin Co, New York, 1993a.

Kohn A, 'Choices for children', *Phi Delta Kappan* 75 (1), pp8–20, 1993b.

Lefever R, *How to Identify Addictive Behaviour,* Promis Books Limited, 1988.

Lefever R, *Inside the Madness,* Promis Books Limited, 1997.

Maslow AH, 'A Theory of Human Motivation', *Psychological Review* 50, pp370–96, 1943.

Napier R & Gershenfeld M, *Group Theory and Practice,* Houghton Mifflin Company, Boston, 1985.

O'Donnell DJ, 'History of the growth of the Institute for Reality Therapy', *Journal of Reality Therapy* 8, pp2–8, 1987.

Palmer B & Palmer, K, *The Successful Meeting Master Guide,* Prentice-Hall, Englewood Cliffs, NJ, 1983.

Pask G, *The Cybernetics of Learning & Performance,* Hutchinson, London, 1976.

Powers W, *Behavior, the Control of Perception,* Aldine, New York, 1973.

Rand A, *The Fountainhead,* New American Library, New York, 1943.

Sickles W, *Psychology: a Matter of Mind,* Kendall/Hunt, Dubique, Iowa, 1976.

Steltzer L, *Paradoxical Strategies in Psychotherapy,* John Wiley & Sons, New York, 1986.

Weeks G & L'Abate L, *Paradoxical Psychotherapy,* Brunner/Mazel, New York, 1982.

Whitehouse D, 'Adlerian antecedents to Reality Therapy and Control Theory', *Journal of Reality Therapy* 3, pp10–14, 1984.

Wiener N, *Cybernetics,* John Wiley & Son, New York, 1948.

Wiener N, *The Human Use of Human Beings: Cybernetics & Society,* Mifflen, Boston, 1950.

Wubbolding RE, 'Reality Therapy as an antidote to burn out', *American Mental Health Counsellors Association Journal* 1, pp39–43. 1979.

Wubbolding RE, 'Reality management: getting results', *Landmark,* Indo American Society, Bombay, India, 11, pp6–8, 1984.

Wubbolding RE, 'Reality Therapy applied to alcoholism', *The Counsellor* 1, pp5–6, 1985.

Wubbolding RE, *Reality Therapy Training Manual,* Center for Reality Therapy, Cincinnati, 1986.

Wubbolding RE, 'A model for group activities related to teaching Reality Therapy', *Journal of Reality Therapy* 6(2), pp23–28, 1987.

Wubbolding RE, *Using Reality Therapy,* HarperCollins, New York, 1988.

Wubbolding RE, *A set of directions for putting (and keeping) yourself together,* Center for Reality Therapy, Cincinnati, 1990a.

Wubbolding RE, *Reality Therapy and family counseling,* Center for Reality Therapy, Cincinnati, 1990b.

Wubbolding RE, *Managing people: what to say when what you say doesn't work,* Center for Reality Therapy, Cincinnati, 1990c.

Wubbolding RE, *Understanding Reality Therapy,* HarperCollins, New York, 1991.

Wubbolding RE, *Managing the Disruptive Classroom,* Agency for Instructional Television, Bloomington, Indiana, 1993.

Wubbolding RE, 'Reality Therapy: what is it?', *Journal of the British Association for Counselling* 5, pp117–119, 1994.

Wubbolding RE, *Reality Therapy Training Manual* (9th revision), Center for Reality Therapy, Cincinnati, 1996.

Wubbolding RE, *Doing Reality Therapy* (in preparation).

***For information on Reality Therapy,
its Certification Programme or short workshops,
please contact:***

John Brickell
Centre for Reality Therapy (UK)
PO Box 193
Romsey
Hampshire
SO51 6YE
United Kingdom

Tel: +44 (0) 1794 885 898
Fax: +44 (0) 1794 885 899
Email: realchoiceuk@aol.com

The William Glasser Institute (UK)
'Brocklands'
Romsey Road
Whiteparish
Near Salisbury
Wiltshire
SP5 2TE
United Kingdom

Tel & Fax: +44(0) 1794 884215
http://www.williamglasserinstitute.uk.com

Linda Harshman
The William Glasser Institute
22024 Lassen St, Suite 118
Chatsworth
California 91311
United States of America

Tel: (818) 700 8000
Fax (818) 700 0555